D0174742

Dr. Mohler gives a fresh and encouraging word on the God who still speaks and a people who must obey, as he takes us on an expositional journey through the Ten Commandments. You will be well reminded that "God speaks in the fire and through His son."

> **Johnny Hunt**
> Senior pastor of First Baptist Church of Woodstock, Georgia,
> and president of the Southern Baptist Convention

Al Mohler is a like a biblical prophet of old speaking into a modern-day wilderness of confusion and compromise. In this exposition of the Ten Commandments, he is following in a train of faithful Christian ministers who used the ten words (along with the Apostles' Creed and the Lord's Prayer) to teach "Christianity 101." But there are riches here for those both new to and mature in the faith. Read and grow.

> **Ligon Duncan**
> Senior minister, First Presbyterian Church,
> Jackson, Mississippi

In our noisy culture, voices of all kinds are bombarding us. In Al Mohler's book *Words from the Fire*, he challenges us to hear the voice of God roaring from the fire. God's Word to us through the Ten Commandments is clear, convicting, and compelling. This incredible read will silence the noise around you and call you to hear the only voice that leads you to a life of holiness. Get this book, read it, share it, teach it, and give another copy of it to a friend.

> **Ronnie W. Floyd**
> Senior pastor, First Baptist Church of Springdale
> and The Church at Pinnacle Hills, Arkansas

I love how my friend Al Mohler instills in *Words from the Fire* a sense of reverence, respect, and mystery at the awesomeness of God's truth proclaimed to God's people. Something's going on that is so much bigger than you and me. "We have this treasure in earthen vessels, so that the surpassing greatness of the power will be of God and not from ourselves" (2 Corinthians 4:7). This reminder will never grow old.

> **James MacDonald**
> Senior pastor of Harvest Bible Chapel

San Diego Christian College
2100 Greenfield Drive
El Cajon, CA 92019

This is a rare book of deep scriptural insight combined with acute cultural analysis. Dr. Mohler helps us see that, far from being simply "rules" about Christian living, these Ten Commandments embody the heart of Christian faith. Serious Christians, pastors, teachers, and all those wishing to understand the urgent relevance of this ancient code for today's confused world will greatly benefit from this book.

J.D. Greear
Lead pastor, the Summit Church, Raleigh-Durham, N.C.

Dr. Mohler has admirably achieved the difficult task of being both faithful to Holy Scripture and relevant to the cultural crises of our day. These essays take God's timeless Ten Commandments and apply them in an inspiring and timely way to the moral crises of our current culture.

Dr. Richard Land
President of The Ethics & Religious Liberty Commission of the Southern Baptist Convention

Of the myriad of books written on the Ten Commandments, I put Al Mohler's up there close to the top of the list. It is contemporary, insightful, interesting, and above all *biblical*. If you want a fresh but thoroughly Christian perspective on the BIG TEN, here it is!!

Phil Roberts
President of Midwestern Baptist Theological Seminary

If we are to know God, He must speak—and He has! In *Words From The Fire*, Al Mohler Jr. carefully and clearly reveals to us the God who spoke in the Ten Commandments. This book is exegetically sound and theologically solid. I never hear or read Al that I am not blessed and challenged. Reading this book was no exception.

Dr. Daniel L. Akin
President, Southeastern Baptist Theological Seminary

"A lion has roared; who will not fear? The Lord God has spoken; who can but prophesy?" (Amos 3:8). In his new book, *Words from the Fire*, Al Mohler, like Amos, reminds us that God's revealed Word in Scripture, specifically in the Decalogue, changes everything for everyone! By His grace, God has spoken His Word. We ignore it or disobey it at our own peril. But if we obey it, our lives are blessed. This work is a welcomed breath of fresh air in our day of self-centered, anti-authoritarian relativism. I commend it wholeheartedly.

Steve Gaines, PhD
Senior pastor, Bellevue Baptist Church, Memphis, Tennessee

241.52
M 698w

20.23

R. ALBERT MOHLER, JR.

WORDS
FROM THE
FIRE

HEARING THE VOICE OF GOD
IN THE 10 COMMANDMENTS

MOODY PUBLISHERS
CHICAGO

© 2009 by
R. ALBERT MOHLER JR.

All rights reserved. No part of this book may be reproduced in any form without permission in writing from the publisher, except in the case of brief quotations embodied in critical articles or reviews.

All Scripture quotations, unless otherwise indicated, are taken from *The Holy Bible, English Standard Version*. Copyright © 2000; 2001 by Crossway Bibles, a division of Good News Publishers. Used by permission. All rights reserved.

Scripture quotations marked NASB are taken from the *New American Standard Bible®*. Copyright © 1960, 1962, 1963, 1968, 1971, 1972, 1973, 1975, 1977, 1995 by The Lockman Foundation. Used by permission. (www.Lockman.org)

Scripture quotations marked NKJV are taken from the *New King James Version*. Copyright © 1982 by Thomas Nelson, Inc. Used by permission. All rights reserved.

Scripture quotations marked KJV are taken from the King James Version.

Interior Design: Ragont Design
Cover Design: brandnavigation.com
Cover Image: iStock

Library of Congress Cataloging-in-Publication Data

Mohler, R. Albert
 Words from the fire : hearing the voice of God in the Ten commandments
/ R. Albert Mohler Jr.
  p. cm.
 ISBN 978-0-8024-5488-1
 1. Ten commandments. 2. Christian life--Baptist authors. I. Title.
 BV4655.M48 2009
 241.5'2--dc22

                              2009019929

This book is printed on acid free recycled paper containing 30% PCW (Post Consumer Waste) and manufactured in the United States of America by Thompson Shore.

We hope you enjoy this book from Moody Publishers. Our goal is to provide high-quality, thought-provoking books and products that connect truth to your real needs and challenges. For more information on other books and products written and produced from a biblical perspective, go to www.moodypublishers.com or write to:

Moody Publishers
820 N. LaSalle Boulevard
Chicago, IL 60610

1 3 5 7 9 10 8 6 4 2

Printed in the United States of America

*D*edicated to my precious family. To my wife, Mary, without whom nothing would be written, nothing done. Her care for me is a magnificent manifestation of God's love. Her love for us all is precious and ever inspiring. Her intelligence and wisdom are legendary. To Katie, who brightens every day and brings delight to her father and mother. Shine on, sweet daughter. To Christopher, who helps me to see what I never would otherwise have seen and to think what I would otherwise never have thought. Way to go, son. They, along with Baxter, the faithful and happy beagle, make our home a place of priceless joy. I am a man most blessed.

The Master hath called us,
The children who fear Him,
Who march 'neath Christ's banner,
His own little band.

Contents

Acknowledgments

$\mathcal{A}$ book may be written in solitude, but it is never a solitary endeavor. Even as we ourselves are walking collectives of conversations, books, thoughts, sermons, songs, and impressions—any book reflects far more than the work of its author. I am especially aware of that truth as I express appreciation to many who were especially helpful with respect to this book. First, I want to thank the Southern Seminary family for listening to the sermons that form the foundation for this project. I am ever thankful for the opportunity of working with this faculty, these students, and the larger family of The Southern Baptist Theological Seminary and Boyce College. I especially want to thank Scott Lamb, director of research in the Office of the President, who has contributed so much to the management of this project. I deeply appreciate both his labor and his heart. Two others, Jason Allen and Matt Hall, have protected my time for this project and so many others in their role as executive assistant to the president. Justin Leighty helped me immensely with the organization of bibliographic materials. Interns David Dewberry, Drew Griffin, Ryan Helfenbein, Trent Hunter, Cody King, and Tyler Smith add energy and insight to my daily work, including writing projects.

Robert Wolgemuth, my literary agent, is a man of rare giftedness, invaluable experience, and kind friendship. Dave DeWit at Moody Publishers is always helpful, insightful, and encouraging. I also want to thank his colleagues Jim Vincent and Pam Pugh.

I am deeply indebted to my parents, Dick and Janet Mohler, who raised me in a Christian home and had me at church whenever the doors were open. In this warm and nurturing context, I first learned and loved the Ten Commandments. Finally, I'm always indebted to my sweet family, to whom this book is dedicated. As with every other dimension in my life, they are in this book, too. Their encouragement and love are priceless.

Indeed, ask now concerning the former days which were before you, since the day that God created man on the earth, and inquire from one end of the heavens to the other. Has anything been done like this great thing, or has anything been heard like it? Has any people heard the voice of God speaking from the midst of the fire, as you have heard it, and survived? Or has a god tried to go to take for himself a nation from within another nation by trials, by signs and wonders and by war and by a mighty hand and by an outstretched arm and by great terrors, as the Lord your God did for you in Egypt before your eyes? To you it was shown that you might know that the Lord, He is God; there is no other besides Him. Out of the heavens He let you hear His voice to discipline you; and on earth He let you see His great fire, *and you heard His words from the midst of the fire*. Because He loved your fathers, therefore He chose their descendants after them. And He personally brought you from Egypt by His great power, driving out from before you nations greater and mightier than you, to bring you in and to give you their land for an inheritance, as it is today. Know therefore today, and take it to your heart, that the Lord, He is God in heaven above and on the earth below; there is no other. So you shall keep His statutes and His commandments which I am giving you today, that it may go well with you and with your children after you, and that you may live long on the land which the Lord your God is giving you for all time.

〜 Deuteronomy 4:32–40 (NASB, italics added)

Introduction

"Has Any People Heard the Voice of God Speaking . . . and Survived?"

One of the great touchstone passages in all Scripture appears in Deuteronomy 4. My heart and soul are absolutely struck by the question—a rhetorical question, but a very real question asked in verse 33: "Has any people heard the voice of God speaking from the midst of the fire, as you have heard it, and survived?"(NASB).

Just like the Israelites at Mount Sinai, we are summoned together as God's people—to speak of God, to sing about God, to worship God. It is no small thing to dare to speak of God. We actually claim that we teach what God has taught.

There ought to be a bit of humility in recognizing the audacity of that claim. It would be a baseless claim—an incredible claim—if God has not spoken from the midst of the fire and allowed us to hear. On what authority do we speak? Is it the authority of the churches of our respective denominations? Such authority is no small thing, but is still not enough.

To dare speak of these things, we invoke the authority of God, for He alone could reveal Himself, speak these things, and tell us what we must know.

The great philosophical crisis of our day is an epistemological crisis—a crisis of knowing and a crisis of knowledge. It is a challenge for the Christian thinker, the Christian theologian, the Christian minister, the Christian preacher, and the Christian institution—the whole of Christianity. The crisis can be summed up in one question: How do we know and teach what we claim to know and teach?

Francis Schaeffer well understood the epistemological crisis and accordingly titled his most significant contribution, *He Is There and He Is Not Silent*. I first read this classic as a sixteen-year-old. To be honest, I think the greatest assurance I got from the book at that age was that some really smart person believed in God. But even at that age, lacking the vocabulary to understand what I was experiencing, I understood the epistemological crisis. How do we know anything? How would we speak of anything? Furthermore, how do we jump from the empirical knowledge of what we can observe to speaking of God whom we cannot see?

A NEW LEAP IN AUDACITY

The claim to know anything, certainly in terms of empirical and scientific observation and study and phenomenology, is audacious enough. But then to speak of the "immortal invisible God only wise"—that is a new leap of audacity altogether.

Dr. Schaeffer understood the epistemological problem that is silence—the claim and the implication that we can know nothing. And he understood that there is only one epistemological answer—revelation. Christianity depends upon a Christian epistemology, a Christian theory of knowledge based in revelation alone. There is no greater challenge than this—to make certain we know on what authority we speak, and know, and teach.

In Deuteronomy 4, Moses reminds Israel of the authority by which they were to live. They heard the voice of God speaking from the midst of the fire and survived. This great sermon concludes the introductory section to Deuteronomy, and stands as a unit all to itself. The sermon begins and ends with a parallel structure, and in the midst is itself a large component of a suzerainty treaty. Such a treaty was a common form in the ancient Near Eastern world, giving the conqueror the right to set down the terms of the treaty. In the book of Deuteronomy, the conqueror is none other than the Lord God Jehovah and the conquered is none other than His own chosen nation Israel. God sets down terms, and they are very easy to understand. It comes down to a very simple formula: hear and obey and live. Refuse to hear, disobey, and bear the wrath of God.

Looking back to the covenant at Horeb, it is clear that obedience led to blessing, disobedience led to God's curse. The generations that survived, kept alive through forty years of wandering in the wilderness, witnessed the death of their own parents who disobeyed and did not trust the Lord.

And now, as the Lord prepares His people for the conquest of the Holy Land, they hear exhortation and memory mixed together. Lest they forget, they are being reminded that they heard the voice of God speaking from the midst of the fire and survived. They share in the memory of God's great saving work in bringing Israel out of captivity to Pharaoh in Egypt, and His keeping the children of Israel alive through forty years of wandering in the wilderness. They were led by smoke and by fire—Moses says, "Remember, and live!"

THESE TEN WORDS

Deuteronomy, *deutero nomos*, means the second giving of the law, because Deuteronomy 5 again contains the Ten Commandments, *these Ten Words*. The theme is very clear. Israel, in terms of its elect status, is the chosen nation of God. The Torah serves as a constant reminder of their special status. In these Ten Words, the central truth is that the Lord God spoke to His people, they heard, and they survived. Looking backward to Deuteronomy 4:10–11, Moses says:

Remember the day you stood before the Lord your God at Horeb, when the Lord said to me, "Assemble the people to Me, that I may let them hear My words so they may learn to fear Me all the days they live on the earth, and that they may teach their children." You came near and stood at the foot of the mountain, and the mountain burned with fire to the very heart of the heavens: darkness, cloud and thick gloom. (NASB)

We must remind ourselves that the giving of the Ten Commandments cannot be separated from the narrative context from which it comes. The propositional truth so clearly there in the law, comes in the midst of a history of a people and God's dealing with the people. *It is a relational revelation,* and it is a dramatic revelation. Israel is reminded not only of what they heard, but of the context in which they heard it:

The mountain burned with fire to the heart of heaven, wrapped in darkness, cloud, and gloom. Then the Lord spoke to you out of the midst of the fire. You heard the sound of words, but you saw no form—only a voice. So He declared to you His covenant which He commanded you to perform, that is, the Ten Commandments, and wrote them on two tablets of stone. (Deuteronomy 4:11–13 NASB)

"The Lord spoke to you out of the midst of the fire," Moses said. "You heard the sound of words, but saw no form; there was only a voice."

THE SILENT IDOLS, THE SPEAKING GOD

A voice! As will be made clear in the Second Commandment—this is not a God who is seen, but a God who is heard. The contrast with the idols is very clear—the idols are seen, but they don't speak. The one true and living God is not seen, but He is heard. The contrast is intentional, graphic, and clear—we speak because we have heard. And the voice of God is not something Israel deserved, nor do we. It is sheer mercy.

We have no right to hear God speak. We have no call upon His voice. We have no right to demand that He would speak. We are accustomed to pointing to the cross of Christ and glorying in the cross of Christ —as we ought always to do—and saying of the cross, "There is mercy!" But at Mount Horeb, there too was mercy! There is mercy when God speaks. This is the mercy of God allowing us to hear His voice.

I think there is the danger that contemporary evangelicals think of the doctrine of revelation primarily as an epistemological problem. Even those who hold to a high doctrine of Scripture, affirming the inerrancy of Scripture, verbal inspiration, and propositional truth are still in danger of thinking of revelation primarily in epistemological terms. The reality is that revelation is mercy, a gift. As Professor Eugene Merrill has said more specifically, speaking of Deuteronomy 4:33, no people other than Israel has ever heard God speak out of the fire and lived to tell about it. The fact is, as Professor Merrill said, there are not even any other peoples that heard the voice of the Lord speak out of the fire and *didn't* live to tell about it.[1] The Lord God spoke uniquely and particularly to Israel, but knowing the speaker and understanding who He is, the miracle is that even those He would allow to hear His voice would survive.

The background, of course, is the paganism of that day. The idols were many, but the idols were silent. The silence of the idols is a pervasive biblical theme. Think of 1 Kings 18, and the battle of the gods. Think of Elijah as he waits and watches the prophets of Asherah and Baal. Watch as the prophets of Baal jump around the altar and lacerate their bodies so that the blood flows down into the ground, and they leap to get Baal's attention. But, as we are told in 1 Kings 18, there was no voice. No one answered, no one paid attention. Idolatry is contrasted with the religion of Israel on the basis of revelation. The idols do not speak. The Lord God of Israel does. The idols are seen but not heard. God is heard but not seen.

The background of this, of course, is the horrible thought that must be in the background of our thinking and in the foreground of our hearts. What if God had not spoken? What if we ourselves had not received this inheritance through Israel's gift? A part of what it means to be engrafted upon the tree, the wild olive branch, is that this too is the word of God to us.

What if God had not spoken? If God had not spoken, the seminary I lead would not exist, at least not along the same lines. If God had not spoken, we might still have a school of religion. Human beings, in the blindness of trying to figure things out, would come to some notion of transcendence and even think up arguments for the existence of a deity. Pondering long enough on an argument from design, we could come to a "watchmaker" thesis, bringing an explanatory matrix to all we see.

Of course, we need not speak hypothetically about this. All we have to do is listen in on the cultural chatter, and we can hear the kind of conversation that would take place if God had indeed not spoken. Just visit some of the more liberal divinity schools, theological seminaries, and universities. There you will hear the kind of philosophical discourse, teaching, and worldview that would emerge *everywhere* if God had not spoken.

Such purveyors of so-called knowledge would lead us to ask: what if this is all really just a game we are playing, each using whatever language game is convenient and handy in terms of our social and cultural and linguistic system? They reason that if all this really is something of a smorgasbord of worldviews, then we can put it all together as best we see fit. If God had not spoken, then there is no end to that game. If God has not spoken, then there is no one who is right, and there is no one who is wrong. If God has not spoken, then all you have is the end game of postmodernism—nihilism without knowledge.

IF GOD HAS SPOKEN . . .

But if God *has* spoken, everything is changed. If God has spoken, then the highest human aspiration must be to hear what the Creator has said. And though the revelation of God is not merely propositions, it is never less than that. Revelation is personal. Hearing the voice of the Lord God is not merely to receive information, but to meet the living God. We are accustomed to speaking and singing of the grace and mercy of God, and of our redemption in the cross of Christ. But we must also speak of the mercy of God in revelation.

In the book of Deuteronomy, we meet the speaking God. Again, in verse 33: "Has any people heard the voice of God speaking from the midst of the fire, as you have heard it, and survived?"(NASB). Mercy and grace meet here—also, as Moses makes clear, this text affirms accountability. This is, in its own way, a *protogospel*, a revelation of the law, a discontinuity or distinction, but a continuity all the same, law and gospel. Christopher Wright, commenting on what took place at Sinai, said that what really mattered there was not that there had been a theophonic manifestation of God, but that there had been a verbal revelation of God's mind and will. Sinai was a cosmic audiovisual experience, but it was the audio that mattered. It is the audio that matters, for God has spoken.[2]

If God has spoken, let me suggest several realities that should frame our thinking. First, *if God has spoken, we do know*. As a matter of fact, if God has spoken, we *must* know. And what we know, because God has revealed Himself to us, is the highest and the greatest knowledge that any human ear can ever hear. And having heard it, we cannot feign ignorance, acting as if we do not know. That is why Francis Schaeffer said that for the Christian who understands the doctrine of revelation, there is no real epistemological crisis. There is only a spiritual crisis. All that remains is whether you will obey.[3] Also, because we know, there is a firm basis to our life and ministry. We have an authority for our preaching and our teaching. We're not making this up as we go along! Because we have heard, we cannot feign ignorance, and we are accountable for the hearing.

If we are to know Him, He must speak— and He has!

Second, *if God has spoken, we know only by mercy*. There is no pride in our knowing, because everything we know is known by mercy. Carl F. H. Henry describes this mercy of revelation, by speaking of it as, "God's willful disclosure, whereby He forfeits His own personal privacy that His creatures might know Him."[4]

We have no claim upon God and there is no way that we could ever figure Him out. If we are to know Him, He must speak—and He has! In the third volume of his magisterial *God, Revelation and Authority*, Henry said this:

> If divine revelation in terms of speech means anything, it implies among other things that God need not have thus disclosed Himself. God might indeed have remained silent and incommunicative in relation to His creatures; His revelational speech to mankind is not an . . . inevitability of the ultimate nature of things. . . . God's speaking is a venture of divine determination and initiative. It is not to be likened to the mathematically quite predictable spurting of the geyser Old Faithful; instead, like an enigmatic weather pattern, its performance cannot be charted in advance, and in crucial ways it is once-for-all rather than merely sporadic. Even God's extended and ongoing speech in general or universal revelation is moment by moment, precept by precept, a matter of voluntary divine engagement, an address to mankind that carries ever and anon the utmost urgency.[5]

God mercifully lets His people hear. Thus, intellectual pride is the enemy of any true knowledge of God, any real theological education. There is nothing we can figure out or discover. There is no "Aha!" moment where, in some theological laboratory, a new element of divine truth gets discovered. We know by grace and mercy.

Third, *if God has spoken, we too must speak*. There is a command here to preach and teach. Again and again, Israel receives this order to speak, and in like manner, the church also is under this standing order. We preach and we teach and we speak, because God has spoken. Because God has spoken, we dare not remain silent. There is a task here. There is urgency here. We are to be the speaking people of a speaking God. The people of God are *not* to be marked by their silence, but by their speech.

Throughout the warp and woof of Scripture, this teaching mandate is constant. If we skip two chapters forward to Deuteronomy 6, we see Israel being reminded of the responsibility of parents to teach their children. In Nehemiah 8, the importance of this was made clear as Ezra and his colleagues read the text aloud and explained its meaning to the congregation. For the church, the command is just as clear. We are to set forth the truth and make it plain, because if God has spoken, we too must speak.

Fourth, *if God has spoken, then it is all about God, and it is all for our good.* You see, God does speak words of judgment in the Scripture, and God does speak words of warning. Indeed, there are hard words in Scripture, but it is all for our good! God spoke to Israel even the words of warning, in order that Israel might hear the warnings, obey the word, and not suffer the inevitable consequences of disobedience. It is all for our good, every single word. That is why in Deuteronomy 4 we are warned not to add to these words or take away from these words. They are all for our good, like medicine for the soul and food for the body.

> *Indeed,* there are hard words in Scripture, but it is all for our good!

Fifth, *if God has spoken, it is for our redemption.* When we think of the work of God in our salvation, we focus of course in the culmination and the fulfillment of God's saving work in the accomplished work of Christ on the cross. But to read the Scripture is to understand that God has been a redeeming saving God from the very beginning— taking Israel out of Egypt was redemption. Keeping Israel alive, even in the wilderness, was redemption. Speaking to Israel and letting Israel hear and survive was redemption.

Jonathan Edwards well understood this. Speaking of this passage, he says the following:

> This was quite a new thing that God did towards this great work of redemption. God had never done anything like it before. "Did ever people hear the voice of God speaking out of the midst of the fire and live? Or has God assayed to go and take Him a nation that the Lord your God did for you in Egypt?" This was a great advancement of the work of redemption that had been begun and carried out from the fall of man, a great step taken in divine providence towards a preparation for Christ's coming in the world, in working out His great and eternal redemption. For this was the people of whom Christ was to come, and now we see, we may see how that plant flourished that God had planted in Abraham.[6]

God allowing Israel at Horeb, and thereafter, to hear and to survive, was a part of His work of redemption—and revelation is for our redemption, we need to remember that. So often, I think even evangelical Christians speak of revelation at times as if it is something that witnesses to redemption, but it is also a part of God's work of redemption in and of itself, for without revelation, we would not know. We would have no clue. But we do know.

Sixth, *if God has spoken, we must obey*. This is not a word submitted for our consideration. The living God allows us to hear the voice of God from the fire and survive. It is because He has demands to make of us, as Creator speaks to His creatures. And in the giving of the Torah, and the entire body of law and statute and command, there is the requirement of obedience, and it is repeated over and over again. It is stated in principle form, as Israel is told, "If you obey, you will be blessed and you will live. You will prosper in the land that I am giving you." It is in the negative. "If you disobey, you will be cursed. You will bear My wrath. The nations of the world will cast you out. You will go out before them, to be taken as their exiles. You will be cast out of the land."

The demand of obedience is very clear, and it is central to

Deuteronomy 4. Even as the Lord God through Moses is preparing His people to enter the Promised Land, and in order to prepare them is getting ready to recite again the law, these Ten Words—the Ten Commandments—He is saying to them, "Look, it is about obedience. I'm not giving you this information. I'm not letting you hear my voice for your intellectual stimulation. It is not so that you will have an epistemological advantage over the pagan peoples around you! I am allowing you to hear my voice so that you may hear and then obey."

Seventh, *if God has spoken, we must trust.* "Trust and obey, for there is no other way to be happy in Jesus, but to trust and obey."[7] We know that song, or at least some previous generations knew that song. But it really is a matter of trust. Because of the spirit of the age and because of the imperative of the health of the church, we must fashion a clear defense of Scripture in terms of its inspiration and authority and perfection. We must teach that truth, remind ourselves of that truth, and be accountable to that. But in the end, it all comes down to trust—a hermeneutic of trust, an epistemology of trust, a spirituality and theology of trust.

If God has spoken, we trust His Word because we trust in *Him.* Woe unto anyone who would sow seeds of mistrust or distrust of the Word of God. To fail to trust this Word is, as Israel was clearly told, to fail to trust in God Himself. Truth is the very foundation of a proper Christian apologetic. An apologetic of trust, understands that in the end, the character of God is what anchors, not only our epistemology, but our redemption. This is the hope we have not only in this life, but in the life to come. We heard His voice, we read His Word, and implied in Deuteronomy 4 is the inscripturation, the writing of this Word. It is very clear that this is to be now a word that, having been

> *To* fail to trust this Word is to fail to trust in God Himself.

heard, is now written and is accessible to Israel through the reading of the Word, the Word we trust.

Eighth, *if God has spoken, we must witness*, declaring the revealed truth. Deuteronomy 4 has a counterpart in chapter 30 at the end of the book. As Moses now prepares to die, the Lord speaks, beginning in verse 11, and says the following:

> For this commandment which I command you today is not too dif-ficult for you, nor is it out of reach. . . . But the word is very near you, in your mouth and in your heart, that you may observe it.
>
> See, I have set before you today life and prosperity, and death and adversity; in that I command you today to love the Lord your God, to walk in His ways and to keep His commandments and His statutes and His judgments, that you may live and multiply, and that the Lord your God may bless you in the land where you are entering to possess it. But if your heart turns away and you will not obey, but are drawn away and worship other gods and serve them, I declare to you today that you shall surely perish. You will not prolong your days in the land where you are cross-ing the Jordan to enter and possess it. I call heaven and earth to witness against you today, that I have set before you life and death, the blessing and the curse. So choose life in order that you may live, you and your descendants, by loving the Lord your God, by obeying His voice, and by holding fast to Him. (Deuteronomy 30:11, 14–20 NASB)

Three points jump out at us here—love the Lord your God, obey His voice, and hold fast to Him. But look also in the New Testament at Romans 10:8–17, where the apostle Paul uses this very text from Deuteronomy and says:

> But what does it say? "The word is near you, in your mouth and in your heart"—that is, the word of faith which we are preaching, that if you confess with your mouth Jesus as Lord, and believe in your heart that God raised Him from the dead, you will be saved;

for with the heart a person believes, resulting in righteousness, and with the mouth he confesses, resulting in salvation. For the Scripture says, "Whoever believes in Him will not be disappointed." For there is no distinction between Jew and Greek; for the same Lord is Lord of all, abounding in riches for all who call on Him; for "Whoever will call on the name of the Lord will be saved." How then will they call on Him in whom they have not believed? How will they believe in Him whom they have not heard? And how will they hear without a preacher? How will they preach unless they are sent? Just as it is written, "How beautiful are the feet of those who bring good news of good things!" However, they did not all heed the good news; for Isaiah says, "Lord, who has believed our report?" So faith comes from hearing, and hearing by the word of Christ. (NASB)

So, faith in God comes from hearing the voice of God. Hearing and yet surviving. This too explains why we ourselves believe, for according to the formula and logic of Romans 10, somehow we have heard God's revelation. Not one of us was at Horeb, yet we have heard. Someone had to tell. God spoke, and someone had to speak to us. And as the Word of God makes so very clear, there is the mandate for us to go and to tell. If God has spoken, then we do know. If God has spoken, then we are accountable. If God has spoken, it is by mercy and for our good, and if God has spoken, it comes with a commission and a command, which makes a difference of course in the life of a Christian, who is not only the one who has been saved, but instrumentally and day by day, is the one who was heard.

The difference for the church is that we understand what it means to gather together as the ones who by the grace and mercy of God have heard. Under the authority of the Word we gather. We are not making this up as we go along. Our task is not to go figure out what to teach. Our task is not to figure out where to find meaning in life. It is to be reminded continually that we have heard the voice of God speaking from the fire and have survived, and thus we teach.

This is the mercy of God, to hear and yet survive. It is the mercy by which we live every day and experience every moment and evaluate every truth claim and judge every worldview and preach every sermon. We work and we live under that mercy. I cannot help connecting Deuteronomy 4 with Hebrews 1. The experience of Israel—hearing the Lord God speak from the midst of the fire and yet surviving—ties in so beautifully with the prologue of the book of Hebrews: "Long ago, at many times and in many ways, God spoke to our fathers by the prophets, but in these last days he has spoken to us by his Son, whom he appointed the heir of all things, through whom also he created the world" (verses 1–2).

We are here because God has spoken, not only in the fire, but also in the Son—in whose name we gather as the church and in whose name we serve. The voice at Horeb points to its ultimate fulfillment in the incarnation of Jesus Christ, the Word of God incarnate. For beyond the miracle of Israel hearing God's voice and surviving, we can now know the Word of God made flesh . . . and be saved.

𝒯he TEN COMMANDMENTS

And God spoke all these words, saying, "I am the Lord your God, who brought you out of the land of Egypt, out of the house of slavery.

1. "You shall have no other gods before me.

2. "You shall not make for yourself a carved image, or any likeness of anything that is in heaven above, or that is in the earth beneath, or that is in the water under the earth. You shall not bow down to them or serve them, for I the Lord your God am a jealous God, visiting the iniquity of the fathers on the children to the third and the fourth generation of those who hate me, but showing steadfast love to thousands of those who love me and keep my commandments.

3. "You shall not take the name of the Lord your God in vain, for the Lord will not hold him guiltless who takes his name in vain.

4. "Remember the Sabbath day, to keep it holy. Six days you shall labor, and do all your work, but the seventh day is a Sabbath to the Lord your God. On it you shall not do any work, you, or your son, or your daughter, your male servant, or your female servant, or your livestock, or the sojourner who is within your gates. For in six days the Lord made heaven and earth, the sea, and all that is in them, and rested on the seventh day. Therefore the Lord blessed the Sabbath day and made it holy.

5. "Honor your father and your mother, that your days may be long in the land that the Lord your God is giving you.

6. "You shall not murder.

7. "You shall not commit adultery.

8. "You shall not steal.

9. "You shall not bear false witness against your neighbor.

10. "You shall not covet your neighbor's house; you shall not covet your neighbor's wife, or his male servant, or his female servant, or his ox, or his donkey, or anything that is your neighbor's."

⌒ Exodus 20: 1–17

The FIRST COMMANDMENT

You shall have no other gods before me.

~ Exodus 20:3

1

No Other God, No Other Voice

*W*hy should we turn to the Old Testament? Why should we focus on the Ten Commandments? Romans 15:4 answers the question: "For whatever was written in former days was written for our instruction, that through endurance and through the encouragement of the Scriptures we might have hope." These things written in former days were written for the instruction of the church, that through the Scriptures we might have hope.

To live in this day is to live in an antinomian age, an age that is "against all law." Western society is addicted to minimal law and maximum flexibility. So, when we look at this text and visualize this people standing before this mountain, and when we think about what took place here in the life of Israel as they heard the Lord God deliver His own commands and heard Moses teach them concerning these commands—all this seems so distant and far off.

THE TEN COMMANDMENTS AND MODERN SOCIETY

This mountain, known as Sinai, also as Horeb, seems almost covered by the clouds of the past, even as the mountain itself was on this day covered in smoke and in fire and thunder. The God whom most persons acknowledge insofar as they acknowledge *any* God is not in the main a divine legislator. He is not a lawgiver, not someone they fear lest they break His command. The God who spoke is now dismissed by the millions, by the "enlightened" ones, by the intellectual elite, as a sky god of ancient and now overcome superstition. Antinomian to the core, modern society resists the very notion of a binding authority. After all, who can tell *us* what we must and must not do? Who can tell us how we are to live? Who can tell us whom we are to serve?

And then you turn on the television or look at the newspaper or listen to the Supreme Court and hear controversies over the Ten Commandments. Should they or should they not be posted in public places? The U.S. Supreme Court seems itself to be double-minded on the issue, ruling recently that the posting of the Decalogue in Kentucky was illicit, whereas in Texas it was lawful. Same words, different placement, different context, different ruling, no obvious logic. I will defend the constitutionality of posting the Ten Commandments in a public place. But I find it rather perplexing that many of those who seem most ardently committed to the posting of the Ten Commandments can neither recite them nor honestly affirm that they have taught them to their own children.

So, we first must admit that in our day the Ten Commandments seem to serve something of a symbolic role. We know how many there are, we're just not sure what they are. The amazing thing is that the God who is, has spoken. What people, what nation has heard the voice of the Lord speaking from the fire and yet survived? This nation has. This nation Israel heard the Word of the Lord, received these Ten Words, and survived.

THE TEN COMMANDMENTS AND THE CHRISTIAN

How are we as Christians to understand the Ten Commandments? What is our relationship to this text? What binding authority do these words have upon us? Is there continuity or discontinuity? How are we to understand the operation of the Mosaic covenant in distinction to the covenant of Christ? Is this thus binding upon us, or is it nonbinding? We know what these words meant for Israel, but what do they mean for the church?

Jonathan Edwards acknowledged the difficulty. He said this: "There is perhaps no part of divinity intended with so much intricacy and wherein orthodox divines do so much differ as stating the precise agreement and difference between the two dispositions of Moses and Christ."[1] I want to acknowledge this perplexity, but I want to suggest that the issue is actually less difficult than it may appear. Those who would most ardently stress continuity have to recognize a difference between Israel under the law and the church under the covenant of grace. Those who would most ardently argue for discontinuity have to acknowledge that the law of Christ recapitulates and fulfills and extends the law of Moses, in a different way, in a different context, with a different sense of binding address. Yet in the New Testament, nine of the Ten Commandments are repeated. There is no way fully to resolve this issue.

THE LAW AND GRACE: BEYOND SACRIFICE

It is very important that we understand the distinction between law and grace. But in understanding this distinction, we do not celebrate a lawless grace any more than looking to the Old Testament we should see a graceless law. There is grace in the law. Israel, in hearing the Word of the Lord and receiving these words, received grace! And if we do not understand that, we slander both the Old Testament and the God who spoke to Israel at Horeb.

Just imagine for a moment the grace that is in the law. First, the grace present in the law is in the revelation of what God requires of

His people. How? It is a specific knowledge and not confusion. As Israel entered the land of promise, it would be surrounded by people who were grotesquely confused about what God would demand of His people. The confusion was rampant. Is God primarily a God of power who demands a worship that would exercise that kind of power? Is He like Baal? Is He a male deity of fertility and of power whose voice is understood to speak in the thunder? Does the one true and living God demand human blood to appease Him, as the prophets of Baal believed, slicing open their bodies till blood ran down into the dirt (1 Kings 18:26–29)?

The god Molech's holiness required children up to age two be sacrificed.

Canaanite followers of the Asherah and Ashteroth, female fertility deities, surrounded Israel. Primarily one deity in different forms with different idols, the worship of these deities was laced with sexual and orgiastic confusion. Such perversity explains why God warned Israel to stay away from what happened under the sacred groves of evergreen trees where ritualized prostitution to these idols took place. Is that what Israel was to do?

Perhaps the most frightening religious confusion among the nations surrounding Israel was the worship of the god Molech, a god defined in terms of a holiness and anger that required innocent humans to be sacrificed for human guilt. Thus, infants and children up to about the age of two were sacrificed, burned alive on the altar of a lifeless idol. A few years ago, in extending the runway at the Damascus Airport, workers found a pit of burned infant bones, dating back to the time of the Canaanites. These were little skeletons of babies up to about age two, their bodies broken and burned to Molech.[2]

We see then that Israel received such grace at Sinai—grace from the loving and holy God who said, "*This* is what I require of My people. *This* is who I am, and *this* is what My people will look like. Don't slice your bodies. Don't pervert your souls. Don't sacrifice your children. Pay heed to these commandments."

The loving and holy God gave grace, saying, "Don't sacrifice your children. Heed these commandments."

In the restraining power of the law there is grace. We should live every day thankful that God has given this law, written into the cosmos itself and also in His spoken Word (specifically the Pentateuch, the first five books of the Bible). We should be unspeakably thankful for the restraining power of the Law upon the human heart.

THE LAW AND GRACE: THE LAW'S REQUIREMENT FULFILLED IN JESUS

The church also has to look at the written Law as grace in a very different sense, and that is in a pattern of expectation and fulfillment. The Law kills us—it indicts us. As the apostle Paul says, "I would not have known what it is to covet if the law had not said, 'You shall not covet'" (Romans 7:7). But now we know, and knowing this, we must be saved. Who can do this but Jesus Christ? Yes, the Law hurts—even kills—but the Law points to Christ.

There is also grace in the Law, and in the keeping of it. As the Lord God told His people, "For this commandment that I command you today is not too hard for you, neither is it far off" (Deuteronomy 30:11). And, as the message is written into the warp and the woof of the Old Testament, keeping this law leads to prosperity, to longevity, and to happiness.

In looking at this law and looking at the gospel, we understand that there are two different covenants, but one redeeming God, who is constant. We are told that the Law was made necessary by sin. Before the fall, Adam and Eve needed no Ten Commandments. There, the law was perfectly written on the heart and perfectly understood. Before the fall, there was no need for the restraining and teaching powers of the law. But after the fall, we desperately need legislation—written laws that can be known.

Even before the Lord gave *these Ten Words*, there was law. We read about Old Testament patriarchs—men like Abraham and Enoch—men who pleased God. But they didn't please God simply by thinking themselves to be pleasing to God. Rather, they pleased God because their lives comported with that which God commanded. They were not perfect, but they were shaped by a law they understood. As Paul writes in Romans 1, it is a law to which we are all accountable.

Back at the mountain, through the prophet Moses, we confront this grace and revelation of the speaking God who gives these Ten Words. What drama there is—smoke, mountain, lightning, cloud, noise. We cannot sever this text from its canonical context. We dare not take it out of its placement in covenantal history nor out of the narrative in which it is placed. These are not just ten abstract commandments. These are ten words of grace and law addressed to God's elect nation, Israel. We have to read the Ten Commandments remembering the smoke upon the mountain that was shaking. We have to remember even the fear of Israel that resulted from knowing that God had spoken to them at all, much less in the form of these specific words. God revealed Himself in the most personal terms.

But then, we contrast this with the radically new covenant, the new law of Christ, and the new heart through the work of Christ. This is the law perfectly fulfilled in Christ and in His accomplished work. We are now no longer under the law of Moses. But that does not mean that we are no longer taught by the Law.

The apostle John wrote, "For the law was given through Moses; grace and truth came through Jesus Christ"(John 1:17). Christ too was a legislator, declaring His own very clear legislation in the Sermon on the Mount. You are familiar with the formula, "You have heard it said . . . , but I say to you." In those words is fulfillment.

Jesus does not lessen the force of the Law; He heightens it, taking it from mere exteriority into interiority. Murder is rooted in anger, and adultery is rooted in lust. As Christians, we speak of being under the law of Christ, under the new covenant, under the law that is given by Christ and to Christ's people.

THE LAW'S ROLE AS TEACHER

So, how are Christ's people to understand the Old Testament law? The Reformers famously debated whether there are two or three uses of the Law. First, both Luther and Calvin accepted the pedagogical use of the Law—it teaches us our sin. We come to know that we have sinned against a holy God, a fact we desperately need to know. Second, the Law has a civil or political use. The divine law underlies and undergirds all political law. It is a law that is revealed in nature, although our sinfulness prevents us from perfectly perceiving it in nature. This law is written in the conscience, but as Paul says in Romans 2, our fallen conscience is an inadequate moral instrument.

Those first two uses of the Law were well understood, but it is the third use—the didactic use of the Law—that became an issue of debate between the followers of Luther and Calvin. The didactic use of the Law asks the question—does the Law *now* teach us? That is, does the Law now teach Christians? Are we to look to the Old Testament in order to see a pattern for godliness, which is to be replicated in us? And the answer has to be, in some form, yes. Calvin clearly affirmed this third use of the Law, and Luther denied it. But as any reading of Luther—his works, sermons, and even his catechisms will indicate, he denied it but he still practiced it. In teaching his children, he taught them the Ten Commandments. In preaching, he preached the Ten Commandments. So, whether or not you want to refer to it as the didactic use of the Law, we know that this law still speaks to us in a pattern that is to encourage us, even as Paul said in Romans 15:4.

In Christ, we who have been the recipients of this new covenant are able to fulfill the Law in a way that Israel was not. That is not because of who we are; it is because of who Christ is. It is not because of our faithfulness, it is because of Christ's faithfulness. So we read the Old Testament law, and the covenant of Moses, and the Ten Commandments all as a word given to God's elect and chosen nation Israel, even as they prepared to enter the Land of Promise.

But the Law is also for our good. It is not that we have no law, for we are under the law of Christ. The last thing we need is an antinomian church in the midst of an antinomian age. We look back to read these texts in order that the Holy Spirit would apply these words to our heart. We hear the binding address of these words, even as we turn to the New Testament to discern how to apply these things in our own times and in our own lives. On the other hand, the church has often been seduced by legalism and moralism. We must not confuse the gospel with any idea that the law can save us, or that our mission is to see lost persons trust in their moralism.

Exodus 20:1 reminds us, "And God spoke all these words." The divine origin and authorship of the Ten Commandments is paramount. This is not Israel's legislation. The Ten Commandments are not the product of human creativity or a legislative assembly. There is no conference committee at Horeb and Sinai. There is no filibuster, and there is no bill-signing ceremony in the Rose Garden. This is God speaking to His people. There is no negotiation here. This is divine address—"And God spoke all these words."

It is so odd to modern and postmodern minds that we claim a di-

> *The* God who reveals this law reveals Himself. . . . First person intimacy. First person authority.

vine sanction for law. The prevailing secular mind-set says that law is simply a product of human experience codified in legislative form. It is just how we learned to live with each other. There is no absolute or transcendent *ought*. There merely is a phenomenological *is*.

But Israel knows something very different. Because God spoke these words, these are not just ten words, these are *the* Ten Words. Broadcaster Ted Koppel, speaking at Duke University's commencement ceremony several years ago, reminded the students that the Ten Commandments are *not* God's "ten ethical suggestions."[3] This is law. It is command.

And the God who reveals this law also reveals Himself: "I am the Lord your God." First person intimacy. First person authority. He uses the revealed name "I AM." This is a personal and saving Word, identified by the God who situates His own law in His redeeming purpose. Look carefully at the text. "I am the Lord your God." Which God? Who is this God? "Who brought you out of the land of Egypt, out of the house of slavery (Exodus 20:2)."

We must see Christ here as well. We see into the future the Christ who will lead His people out of bondage. Not out of bondage to Pharaoh, but out of bondage to sin. God's constant redeeming purpose is reflected here even in the giving of the law. This is the God who brought Israel out of the land of Egypt, out of the house of slavery, and thus the first command, "You shall have no other gods before me."

THE FIRST COMMANDMENT ASSERTS MONOTHEISM

What does all this mean? First, it means there is one God and only one God. This command begins with the assertion of theism, and not just theism—monotheism. God automatically and necessarily reveals Himself over against the false gods of that day and age, and any other.

A quick survey of modern theology reveals the false gods of our day, not just within the various paganisms, world religions, and forms of blindness, but even inside what is considered the world of Christian theology. All these false gods fall far short of the biblical witness. There is the well-intended deity of American popular culture and the lighter-than-air, dehydrated, just-add-water god of popular imagination. As one author says, this is the "break glass in case of emergency deity."[4] The god of modern theology is finite in so many ways. He is not omnipotent, he is just more powerful than we are. He is not omniscient; he just knows everything that currently may be known—more knowledge than we have. By stark contrast, the infinite God of the Bible is omnipotent, omniscient, omnipresent, self-existent, self-revealing, self-defining, sovereign, and holy. Indeed, the list truly is itself infinite.

John Calvin wrote well when he said that there is a *semenas divinitas*, a seed of divinity, within the human being. This interior knowledge forms part of our conscience and our constitution, being ourselves made in the image of God. It cries out for some object of worship, for we will worship some deity. The only question is—what or *whom* will we worship? In his book *Idols for Destruction*, Herbert Schlossberg says this: "Western society in turning away from the Christian faith has turned to other things."[5] He points out this fact that is often missed—this is not a turning from, it is a turning *to*! This process is commonly called *secularization*, but that only covers the negative aspect. The word connotes the turning away from the worship of God while ignoring the fact that some other deity has taken His place. It is inevitably so.

A.W. Tozer expressed so powerfully this truth when he said, "What comes into our minds when we think about God is the most important thing about us."[6] Several years ago in Britain researchers went door to door asking persons about their belief in God. One of their questions: "Do you believe in a God who intervenes in human history, who changes the course of affairs, who performs miracles, etc.?" When published, their study took as its title the response of one man who was seen as rather typical of those who responded. He answered, "No, I don't believe in *that* God, I just believe in the *ordinary* God."

How many of our friends and neighbors believe in just "the ordinary God"? In listening to evangelicalism, would anyone believe that we worship anything other than an *ordinary* God?

THE FIRST COMMANDMENT
CALLS FOR ULTIMATE ALLEGIANCE

Second, the First Commandment tells us this loving God demands ultimate allegiance—nothing less will do. God's existence defines all reality. If God exists, then everything is now different. As James Orr made clear over a century ago, "This explains the radical antagonism between the two worldviews, one believing in God and one not. Two different starting points for all thought, two different realities—on the one hand silence, on the other hand speech; on the one hand, nihilism, on the other hand, theism, and those in the end are the only two great alternatives."[7]

How do we understand this basic issue today? What is our Canaan? What is our context? Well, look around. We live in the land of idolaters.

Homiletically, it is a challenge to talk about this without being trite, because we at least have to give the tip of the hat to the idolaters of old who knew what they were doing more than the idolaters of late. In the ancient world, at least we knew *who* someone was talking about when they spoke of Baal or Asherah or Moab or Dagon or Zeus or Wotan or Thor or Artemis. They are mostly gone now, but in their place are other idols. There are the idols of religious pluralism around us and the idols of those who don't think themselves religious at all. The idols of self abound; as Oscar Wilde said, "To love oneself is the beginning of a lifelong romance." It is a lifelong romance for just about all of humanity. Those who worship not the one true and living God, eventually worship themselves.

In her book *Smoke on the Mountain*, Joy Davidman, the wife of C. S. Lewis, wrote, "He who is not continually fizzing like champagne with sexual excitement is condemned as a failure in life." She said, "The modern idols are the idols of sex, the state, science, and society." Though speaking a half-century ago, she was right. Sex, the state, science, and society—these are idols of our day. If we are not fizzing like champagne with sexual excitement, if we're not bowing down to the state, if we're not celebrating science and scientism, if we're not finding ultimate meaning in human society, we are written off as simply out of step. Francis Bacon, in his famous aphorism in the *Nova Organum*, said there are four classes of idols: the idols of the tribe, the idols of the cave, the idols of the marketplace, and the idols of the theater. And each is still with us today.

THE FIRST COMMANDMENT COMMANDS EXCLUSIVITY

Third, the loving God demands exclusivity. Here we face the "mono" in monotheism. Some would have you believe that monotheism is just too much to demand. Looking to the experience of Israel, some try to explain that Israel was not even sure about monotheism. Folks like William Barkley try to describe the evolution of Israel's faith from polytheism (many gods) to henotheism (a hierarchy of gods) to monotheism (one god). I love the response of Philip Ryken, who says, very simply, "God has always been a monotheist."[8] In 1 Corinthians 8:4–6, Paul puts monotheism in the Christian context of exclusivity as he says:

> Therefore as to the eating of food offered to idols, we know that "an idol has no real existence," and that "there is no God but one." For although there may be so-called gods in heaven or on earth— as indeed there are many "gods" and many "lords"—yet for us there is one God, the Father, from whom all things and for whom we exist, and one Lord, Jesus Christ, through whom are all things and through whom we exist.

The idol is a nothing, but it is a dangerous nothing.

Monotheism is controversial in the church today, as is the whole idea of exclusivity. There are those who call themselves evangelicals who flirt with various universalisms and inclusivisms. They do so as a way of getting around the awkwardness, the angularity, and the political incorrectness of this exclusivity—the exclusivity not only of Yahweh, but also of Christ as Redeemer.

One God. As we read in the New Testament, there is one Mediator between God and man. "I am the way. . . . No one comes to the Father except through me," Jesus said (John 14:6). Peter declared, "There is no other name under heaven given among men by which we must be saved" (Acts 4:12). Exclusivity is inherent in monotheism, and that is what scares some people.

Gore Vidal, one of the leading lights of the literary left, attacks the very idea of monotheism with his notion of "sky gods." He says the following:

> Now to the root of the matter. The great unmentionable evil at the center of our culture is monotheism. From a barbaric Bronze Age text known as the Old Testament three anti-human religions have evolved, Judaism, Christianity, Islam. They are sky god religions. They are literally patriarchal. God is the omnipotent father, hence the loathing of women for 2000 years in those countries affected by the sky god and its earthly male delegates. The sky god is a jealous god, of course. He requires total obedience from everyone on earth, as he is in place not just for one tribe but for all creation. Those who would reject him must be converted or killed for their own good. Ultimately, totalitarianism is the only sort of politics that can truly serve the sky god's purpose. Any movement of a liberal nature endangers his authority and that of his delegates on earth. One god, one king, one pope, one master in the factory, one father-leader in the family home.[9]

If we do not understand the antipathy toward the very notion of monotheism, we will not understand a significant part of what it means to bear the scandal of the gospel in this generation. Human beings are worshipers. We will worship either the one true and living God, or we will worship an idol of our own devising or our own adoption. We will worship the idol of the tribe or the cave or the marketplace, the theater, or the idol of the self.

"You shall have no other gods before me." This is not a reference to a hierarchy or an issue of preeminence as though God is saying, "I must be the highest of all gods. You must have none other before me."

That is not what this text means at all. Rather, God says in effect, "You dare not bring even the acknowledgment of any other so-called god into my face." No acknowledgment of any other god. This truly is *mono*theism. To understand the very heart of this is to understand, as Calvin wrote his exposition of this text in *The Institutes*, the intended scene. This is like a shameless woman who brings in an adulterer before her husband's very eyes only to vex his mind the more. That is as idolatry in God's eyes.

Luther, explaining what a god is, and thus what an idol is, in contrast explained, in his *Larger Catechism*:

> What is a God? Answer: A God is that to which we look for all good and in which we find refuge in every time of need. To have a God is nothing else than to trust and believe Him with our whole heart. As I have often said, the trust and faith of the heart alone makes both god and idol. If your faith and trust are right, then your God is the true God. On the other hand, if your trust is false and wrong, then you have not the true God.

We have to read this first commandment along with that word that was given to Israel through Moses in Deuteronomy, the *Shema*: "Hear, O Israel: The Lord our God, the Lord is one. You shall love the Lord your God with all your heart and with all your soul and with all your might. And these words that I command you today shall be on your heart" (Deuteronomy 6:4–6). And as our Savior said: "You shall love the Lord your God with all your heart and with all your soul and with all

Who is it in that we truly trust? In answering that question, we find who our God is.

your mind. This is the great and first commandment. And a second is like it: You shall love your neighbor as yourself. On these two commandments depend all the Law and the Prophets (Matthew 22:3–4).

What is it in the end? Who is it in the end that we truly trust and truly adore? For in answering that question, we find who our God is.

For Christian believers, monotheism is fundamental, but not yet complete. In Christ we come to know that the one true God reveals Himself supremely in Christ. The incarnate Christ adds to the scandal of monotheism when He told His disciples, "I am the way, and the truth, and the life. No one comes to the Father except through me" (John 14:6). There is only one God . . . only one Savior . . . only one gospel.

Our understanding of monotheism is fulfilled in Christ. Christianity is not a *mere* monotheism, but a Trinitarian monotheism. In Christ we truly come to know what it means to fulfill the first commandment.

"I am the Lord your God, who brought you out of the land of Egypt, out of the house of slavery. You shall have no other gods before me." And brothers and sisters, we must not. These words, written to Israel of old, are for us, in order that we might be instructed. They are for our instruction that through the encouragement of the Scriptures we might have hope.

The SECOND COMMANDMENT

You shall not make for yourself a carved image, or any
likeness of anything that is in heaven above, or that is in
the earth beneath, or that is in the water under the earth.
You shall not bow down to them or serve them, for I the
Lord your God am a jealous God, visiting the iniquity of the
fathers on the children to the third and the fourth
generation of those who hate me, but showing steadfast
love to thousands of those who love me and keep my
commandments.

～ Exodus 20:4–6

2

The God Who Is Heard and Not Seen

J had been president of the seminary I serve only a short time when I received a phone call from a troubled visitor to our campus. This gentleman had been through the campus center, and called to tell me that we had an idol at Southern Seminary. This was of obvious concern to me, so I left my office to go find the idol.

And I found it! It was as I had been told—an idol, a carved image, immediately recognizable for what it was, on display behind glass, in the campus center of Southern Seminary, a part of a missions collection that had been brought back from a distant nation.

Immediately, I recognized the quandary. This had been brought back by those who meant to contrast the worship of the one true and living God over such empty and vain idols. But it was displayed without explanation. So I did what I felt was my responsibility to do. I found out how to get into this display, and not knowing exactly what one does when one finds an idol on one's campus, I put it behind the display so that it would not be seen.

I was planning to ponder and pray about how to handle this particular problem, when walking through the center the next day I saw that it was back. I repeated my procedure of going into the display and taking the idol down and hiding it behind, only the next day to come back and to find it back in its place again!

I was in a war over the idols with our housekeeping staff. They were wondering who was vandalizing the display; I was ready to declare myself Oliver Cromwell and take matters into my own hands. This idol, dear friends, is gone, but other idols are always near to us.

COMMANDMENT NUMBER ONE OR TWO?

We come to the second commandment in Exodus 20:4–6, which begins, "You shall not make for yourself a carved image, or any likeness of anything that is in heaven above, or that is in the earth beneath, or that is in the water under the earth. You shall not bow down to them or serve them."

Part of the debate in posting the Ten Commandments is this: How does one number them? According to the Reformed tradition, this is the Second Commandment. According to the Roman Catholics and the Lutheran tradition, it is still part of the first commandment, but they then split what we know as the Tenth Commandment into the ninth and the tenth. But I think there is a very clear distinction between what we call the First Commandment and the Second Commandment. The first commands us to worship only the one true God, and the second commands us to worship Him as He would be worshiped.

"You shall not make." The very clarity of that declaration ought to strike us, because we are the beings who make things. And having made things, we take pleasure in them. We can build a house and we can live in it. We can build a boat and we can sail in it. We can build a table and eat at it. We make all kinds of things material and immaterial, and find great pleasure in them.

Therein is the problem, the seduction, and the allure. We are *homo-idolater*, the creature who would fashion our own god. This is the true perennial heresy. East of Eden, isolation is always close at hand. We are natural-born idolaters, and it is good that we admit this up front.

We are natural-born idolaters, and it is good that we admit this up front.

Why are fallen sinful human beings born idolaters? The reason is simple—we must worship, we *will* worship. Even as nature abhors a vacuum, so does the human soul. The human soul will find an object of worship, either on the shelf, on the altar, in the mirror, or in heaven. We are born idolaters.

We confront this, as Paul does in Acts 17, in the graphic picture of this inherent need seen in ancient Athens. Paul is provoked in his spirit as he sees the Athenians and observes their temples and idols and altars. It seemed that every god that was conceivable or had ever been heard of had an altar in Athens. There was even an altar to an unknown god (verse 23). We are natural-born idolaters, and we will commit idolatry. We will worship, even if we do not recognize that we are doing so. The atheist worships the concept of atheism, and all that inevitably follows. To be created in the image of God is to be made a worshiping being.

The allure of idolatry is certainly connected to our creativity and skill. We make objects of art, and then appreciate them. But this command is very clear: "You shall not make for yourself a carved image, or any likeness of anything that is in heaven above, or that is in the earth beneath, or that is in the water under the earth." The two words there—*image* and *likeness*—are similar in the Hebrew, reinforcing each other within this context.

The command prohibits anything that is to attract the eyes in order to seduce the soul. "You shall not make a carved image or any likeness of anything." This is a categorical command against idols. Why? Because, in this very passage, God identifies Himself as a jealous God. He is filled with zeal for His own name, for His own identity, for His own worship. He is a jealous God, who demands a worship that befits His own character and identity.

WHY IDOLS ARE DANGEROUS

So, what is so dangerous about idols? Why is it so important to know how to worship this one true God? Simply put, our worship betrays our theology. To worship the right god in the wrong way is to testify to the wrong god. That is the danger in worship. Through wrong worship, we give testimony to the wrong god. We must not give a false witness to God's character and to His identity and to His purpose and to His will and to His glory. We must memorize this formula, and inscribe it upon our hearts and upon our churches: right God = right worship. The wrong worship implies the wrong god.

British philosopher Roger Scruton writes, "God is defined in the act of worship far more precisely than he is defined by any theology."[1] This an accurate judgment. Watch a people at worship, and you will find out exactly what they believe about God. You may pay attention to their hymnals and to their Scriptures and to all the things that they say and all the things that they pray, but most quintessentially it is not their books on theology that will reveal what they believe; it is their worship.

And wrong worship implies the wrong god—an idol that substitutes for the real God. Every idol not only falls short of the reality of the true God, it lies about Him.

IDOLS IMPLY FINITUDE

Here are the lies of the idols. First, idols imply finitude. An idol is a material thing, and the very "thingness" of the thing reveals its limitation. It is here and it is not there. It is a finite thing. It is a limited thing.

What a poor God substitute. God is indeed infinite in all of His perfections. There is no way that a finite object can be worshiped as an infinite God. The idol is inherently finite. Its finitude is grounded in the fact that it is fabricated (the next lie of the idol). All created things are finite. God alone is infinite. When we speak of an idol, we can say, "There it is." But when we say, "There it is," we mean that it is not in a second place.

God does not invite us to gaze on Him as a thing, but rather to listen to His voice. Yahweh provides no likeness of Himself. He has spoken, He has revealed Himself, and He has defined Himself by perfections. He is "immortal, invisible, God only wise, in light inaccessible, hid from our eyes."[2] This is why the "omni" attributes—omnipresent, omnipotent, omniscient, etc.—and all the other characteristics of God revealed in Scripture are so vital to us, because every single one of them points to the infinitude of God's perfection. He not only *knows*, He knows *all* things. He is not only powerful, He is all-powerful. He is not only holy, He is infinitely holy. He is not only merciful, He is infinitely merciful. He is not only just, He is infinitely just. And the very "thingness" of the idol betrays its finitude.

IDOLS IMPLY FABRICATION

Second, idols imply fabrication. An idol is a fabricated thing, created by some human agent. Thus, the commandment begins, "You shall not make." And we do love to make things! We are makers of things, by nature of our humanity. Put a kid in a sandbox; he will fashion something. Or place Legos in front of a child and watch what she does: she will make something.

Once we make something, we admire it. "I have done this thing. This is the work of my hands." We can even try to dignify it, saying, "We are doing it as an act of our worship! We will build this! We'll fashion this! We'll bring all of our artistic ability to this challenge. We wouldn't bring anything less. We will give this our very best." And having given it our very best, we will admire it and worship it.

But God is not a fabricated deity. There is no assembly required—

there is no assembly possible! Idolatry is absolutely delusional. This is why again and again in Scripture, the one true and living God will say, "I made you! You did not make Me! And I made you in My image. You can't make an image of Me."

This issue of fabrication is very important, because in terms of ideas and hopes and aspirations, this is what the skeptics believe religion is all about. In his book *The Essence of Christianity*, German philosopher Ludwig Feuerbach, called God a projection, a wish-being. Feuerbach understood the very logic of idolatry. He argued that humans project deity and the supernatural onto objects or ideas of their own invention. Feuerbach had it right—at least when it comes to idols. In speaking of idolatry, Feuerbach understood the essence of the problem. When one makes an idol, he creates a thing, and having created it, acts as if it is watching him. He makes an object, pretends that it is conscious, and then believes that it sees him. That is what we do when we speak of God.

If we are not careful, if we are not chastened and disciplined to speak of God only as He would be spoken, and to worship God only as He would be worshiped, then we fall right into Feuerbach's trap. We too make of God a projection, a wish-being.

In line with Feuerbach's critique, we find some of the most incredible satire of idolatry in Scripture. For example, Isaiah the prophet pours out his sarcasm upon idolaters. We read the following:

> All who fashion idols are nothing, and the things they delight in do not profit. Their witnesses neither see nor know, that they may be put to shame. Who fashions a god or casts an idol that is profitable for nothing? Behold, all his companions shall be put to shame, and the craftsmen are only human. Let them all assemble, let them stand forth. They shall be terrified; they shall be put to shame together.
>
> The ironsmith takes a cutting tool and works it over the coals. He fashions it with hammers and works it with his strong arm. He becomes hungry, and his strength fails; he drinks no water and is faint. The carpenter stretches a line; he marks it out with a pen-

cil. He shapes it with planes and marks it with a compass. He shapes it into the figure of a man, with the beauty of a man, to dwell in a house. He cuts down cedars, or he chooses a cypress tree or an oak and lets it grow strong among the trees of the forest. He plants a cedar and the rain nourishes it. Then it becomes fuel for a man. He takes a part of it and warms himself; he kindles a fire and bakes bread. Also he makes a god and worships it; he makes it an idol and falls down before it. Half of it he burns in the fire. Over the half he eats meat; he roasts it and is satisfied. Also he warms himself and says, "Aha, I am warm, I have seen the fire!" And the rest of it he makes into a god, his idol, and falls down to it and worships it. He prays to it and says, "Deliver me, for you are my god!" (Isaiah 44:9–17)

This is insanity and grand self-delusion This man grew the tree, and then cut it down. With half the tree, he did that which makes sense—he made a fire. He warmed himself and baked bread and cooked meat. But in his self-delusion, he then carved out of the other half an idol and said, "You are my god!"

Feuerbach described human projections of deity as "wish-beings." The idol implies fabrication, but the one true God is not fabricated. He is self-existent and not created. One of the perfections of His being is that He is uncreated and self-existent and holy. Christianity requires a clear distinction between the Creator and His creation.

IDOLS IMPLY CONTROL

Third, idols imply control—human control. We can pick an idol up and we can put an idol down. We can move an idol to this place, and then we can remove it to another place. The idol is at our disposal. We can hide it from our sight, or we can put it in the center of the room. We will devise our own worship because we have devised our own god. And here we see the issue, directly, that cuts at human pride. Not only are we told that God does not invite our artistic creativity—that hurts—but we are also told that He will not forfeit His control. He will control me, not like some vain idol. You can fashion an idol, move an idol, put a covering over an idol, topple over an idol, and destroy an idol. But you cannot control God. He is the uncontrollable, the all-powerful. His hand will not be stayed.

The god we can control is no god at all. The god we can conjure, create, and construct is no true deity. The very idea of fabrication reverses the control—the one who fabricates is the one who is in control. But we are not the fabricator, we are the fabricated. We are not the Creator, we are the created. We are not the Creator, we are the creature. And our worship must make that abundantly clear. We are not the maker, we are not the controller; we are the created and we are the possessed. It is the reversal of true worship when you revert to idolatry. God cannot be represented in a picture or in a sculpture, reminded John Calvin, because He has intended His likeness to appear in us.

Where do we find the image of God when we worship? It is not in a thing. The image of God is found in the creation He made in His own image—the human creatures given the capacity to worship. Humans alone can consciously know Him and adore Him and worship Him, and therein alone is His likeness to be found.

IDOLS IMPLY NEED

Fourth, idols imply need. Idols have to be fed and clothed and housed. In fact, most of the worship activity associated with idols centers on their neediness. Travel to a country dominated by these forms of idolatry, and you will see multitudes who give themselves to the service of their idols. They create pagodas and temples and structures that draw attention to this idol—this is their service, their liturgy. The idol must be dusted, and the idol must be cleaned.

Those who worship also bring in food and gifts; they light lamps and burn incense. How sad it is to see those who bring food that could go to the hungry and place it in front of the idol who never chews, who never swallows. By the very act of bringing such things to an idol, the worshiper points to the idol's need. This is the devotion the idol will demand.

In contrast, our liturgy, service, and devotion—our reasonable service and our spiritual worship—is to be as a living sacrifice (Romans 12:1), by the mercy of Christ. We do not bring animal sacrifices; we bring ourselves.

Paul spoke to the idolatrous Athenians on this very subject, contrasting the living God with the lifeless idols. He said: "The God who made the world and everything in it, being Lord of heaven and earth, does not live in temples made by man, nor is he served by human hands, as though He needed anything" (Acts 17:24–25).

We are not here because God needs us or our worship—for He needs nothing. When He glorifies Himself with His people, He does so not out of need, but from the natural outworking of His own glory.

The God of the Bible is a jealous God. He is jealous for His own name and jealous for His own character and jealous for His own glory. After all, who made whom? And who needs whom? Paul said to the Athenians, "Being then God's offspring, we ought not to think that the divine being is like gold or silver or stone, an image formed by the art and imagination of man" (Acts 17:29). That is a stern corrective. That explains why Paul was brought up on charges in Athens—and why during his visit, seeing the priority that people had placed in these idols, said, in essence, "You ought not to think this way."

After all, who made whom? And who needs whom?

Again and again, the Scriptures mock the insanity of idol worship. In 1 Kings 18, the passage often known as "the battle of the gods," Elijah stood against the prophets of idolatry. The priests of Baal have done all they can do, crying out to Baal for hours. But there is no answer, there is no voice. Elijah says to them, in effect, "Well, maybe your god is occupied. Maybe he has turned aside" (see 1 Kings 18:26–27). We must miss not the directness of Elijah's sarcasm as he essentially says, "Maybe your idol has gone to the bathroom." After all, if you're going to feed your idol, perhaps the idol will have other needs as well.

IDOLS IMPLY PROCREATION

There is a fifth problem arising from idolatry, and we must speak honestly of it. Idols imply procreation. If you look in an illustrated encyclopedia and find pictures of many idols, you will find something grotesque and obvious—a perversion of sexuality. There seems to be a direct connection between worship of idols and the perversion of sexuality. Many idols are depicted with enlarged genitalia and exaggerated features. There is no subtlety here. The statues and the images are often profane and pornographic—illustrating exaggerated sexuality, exaggerated physicality, and exaggerated procreative ability. People worshiped these idols for their procreative gift and generative power.

A visit to a historic site like the ruins of Ephesus makes this point clear. The temple of Artemis, goddess of Mount Olympus and daughter of Zeus, was one of the Seven Wonders of the World, with Ionic columns once reaching sixty feet high. In the middle of that ancient pagan temple stood a massive statue of Artemis—complete with grotesque and pornographic features. There can be no doubt what was really being worshiped there.

The worship of the true God must have nothing to do with . . . perverse sexual rituals or sexual power or potency.

But God does not give birth, nor does He sire offspring. God is not a womb, out of which emerges creation. The worship of fertility has no place in Christianity. There is absolutely nothing physical or procreative about Yahweh, the God of Israel, and the Father of our Lord Jesus Christ. Canaanite worship involved pornography and sexual perversion. That is why God warned Israel not to do what is done in what were described as sacred groves under evergreen trees. Israel receives a warning, in the starkest and most honest terms, that the worship of the true God must have nothing to do with these practices. No "sacred" prostitution, no twisted and perverse sexual rituals, no worship of genitalia or sexual power or potency.

But Israel did not always keep this command to shun idols. Thus King Jeroboam instructed the people in pagan worship:

> So the king took counsel and made two calves of gold. And he said to the people, "You have gone up to Jerusalem long enough. Behold your gods, O Israel, who brought you up out of the land of Egypt." And he set one in Bethel, and the other he put in Dan. Then this thing became a sin, for the people went as far as Dan to be before one. He also made temples on high places and appointed priests from among all the people, who were not of the Levites. (1 Kings 12:28–31)

Later, when King Jehu reigned in Israel, he eliminated the Baals and the followers of the Baal; yet he did not fully worship Yahweh. We read this:

> Thus Jehu wiped out Baal from Israel. But Jehu did not turn aside from the sins of Jeroboam the son of Nebat, which he made Israel to sin—that is, the golden calves that were in Bethel and in Dan. . . . Jehu was not careful to walk in the law of the Lord the God of Israel with all his heart. He did not turn from the sins of Jeroboam, which he made Israel to sin. (2 Kings 10:28–29, 31)

That is what you would call a reformation stopped in its tracks. Jehu went so far as to remove Baal, but he did not destroy the golden calves.

The procreative danger of idolatry is present in contemporary feminist theology. The 2006 General Assembly of the Presbyterian Church USA received a report on the Trinity in which the denomination and its churches were encouraged to adopt new triads for worship. No longer just Father, Son, and Holy Spirit, they now recommended new trinities—"Overflowing Font, Living Water, and Flowing River"; "Fire that Consumes, Sword that Divides, and Storm that Melts Mountains." Many triads were suggested, including this one: "Compassionate Mother, Beloved Child, and Life-giving Womb." This is idolatry, pure and simple. This is tantamount to bringing in the Canaanite fertility gods to replace the Trinity of Father, Son, and Holy Spirit.

IDOLS IMPLY PHYSICALITY

Sixth, idols imply physicality. There is shape and form to an idol. However, God makes clear in the Bible that He has no likeness and will not be worshiped in this way. In Deuteronomy 4, when Moses is bringing the people back to Horeb, he says this:

> And you came near and stood at the foot of the mountain, while the mountain burned with fire to the heart of heaven, wrapped in darkness, cloud, and gloom. Then the Lord spoke to you out of the midst of the fire. You heard the sound of words, but saw no form; there was only a voice. (Deuteronomy 4:11–12)

IDOLS IMPLY THE VISUAL

Seventh, idols imply the visual. In contrast to idols that are seen but not heard, we worship a God who is heard yet not seen. Our God is a speaking God who commands that we hear His voice, making no attempt to represent His image. We must admit to ourselves that we live in a day much like the day of the Canaanites. We are attracted by the allure of the visual. We must remind ourselves that when Eve was tempted in the garden, gazing on the fruit that was forbidden, it delighted her eyes.

We like to say, "Seeing is believing." No, it is not. Seeing is *not* believing. As a matter of fact, the most important things are the things not seen. "Faith is the assurance of things hoped for, the conviction of things not seen" (Hebrews 11:1). Over and over again, the Scripture prioritizes and honors the verbal over the visual. As Jesus said to "doubting Thomas," "Have you believed because you have seen me? Blessed are those who have not seen and yet have believed" (John 20:29).

This preferring of the verbal over the visual goes right into our understanding of the authority of Scripture and into the centrality of preaching. There is a loss of confidence in the power of the Word that seems to affect so many pulpits and so many preachers. Author Mitchell Stephens of New York University says, "The image is replacing the word as the predominant means of mental transport."[3] We live in days when the primary and the preeminent means of "mental transport"—the exchange of ideas—is indeed the visual rather than the verbal. But this is to our starvation, not to our enrichment.

The late Neil Postman, in his wonderful book *Amusing Ourselves to Death*, said much the same thing over twenty years ago. He argued that our politics and religion, our news and athletics and education and commerce, have been transformed into congenial adjuncts of show business, largely without protest or even much popular notice. The result is that we are a people on the verge of amusing ourselves to death with the visual. Postman dared even to speak of the second commandment. He said the following:

We are a people on the verge of amusing ourselves to death with the visual.

In studying the Bible as a young man I found intimations of the idea that forms of media favor particular kinds of content, and therefore are capable of taking command of a culture. I speak specifically of the Decalogue, the second commandment of which prohibits the Israelites from making concrete images of anything. The God of the Jews was to exist in the word and through the word, an unprecedented conception requiring the highest order of abstract thinking. Iconography, thus, became blasphemy, so that a new kind of god could enter a culture. People like ourselves who are in the process of converting their word center to an image center might profit by reflecting on this Mosaic injunction.[4]

As well we might. But what is the problem with the visual? As Mr. Postman recognized, the visual displaces the verbal. Once we see, we no longer hear.

CONCLUSION: JUDGMENT AND PROMISE

The Second Commandment is followed by this statement—and warning—from God: "You shall not bow down to them or serve them, for I the Lord your God am a jealous God." He is filled with zeal for His own name. To understand this, you have to understand the marriage metaphor that is already present. As Ray Ortlund Jr. makes so clear, the big problem here is that Israel will commit spiritual adultery.[5]

God is a jealous God. And the threat is very clear: God's judgment will inevitably fall upon the idols and the idolaters. Theology has consequences, and one of these consequences is worship. That is why this commandment remains urgently important for us today. Our theological convictions and our patterns of worship shape generations to come. Getting the worship of God wrong, which implies the wrong God, brings spiritual death to subsequent generations. Just look at those lands that have given themselves for so long to idolatry. Just look at those churches and denominations that have given themselves to false doctrine. Just look at any society that has given itself to false gods. We can see the judgment of God from generation to generation to generation.

But there is also a promise here, and the promise is just as clear. Not only does God visit "the iniquity of the fathers on the children to the third and the fourth generation of those who hate" Him, but He shows "steadfast love to thousands of those who love me and keep my commandments" (Exodus 20:5–6). The steadfast love of God is given to all who come to Him by faith and worship Him in ways that please Him.

> *Every* idol comes down to a love of self.

What do we do with this? Well, in the first place, we had better understand that we are natural-born idolaters. Our hearts are idol-making factories, and this is yet more evidence that we are a fallen race. Idolatry is rooted in the depth of who we are. Augustine got to the very heart of this when he said there are, in the end, only two loves—there is the love of God and there is the love of self. And in the end, every idol comes down to a love of self. We fabricate the idol, we fashion it, we feed it, we control it, we admire its beauty and its finitude, for it in the end is *us*. There we are, as idolaters.

What does this say about our worship? We must be very careful that the visual never eclipses the verbal. We must be very careful not to allow things of visual beauty to become the objects of our worship, because they lie; they lie because they cannot represent the infinite beauty of God.

We are to make no image of Him. We should paint no pictures of Him. If we were to know the visual image of Christ, He would have left us His visual image. He did not. And every picture or portrait of Him is an invention, and as an invention, it robs Him of His glory. The worship of icons is just wrapped up in the foolishness of the same lie. God does not command or authorize the use of images in order to understand and worship Him. As a matter of fact, God condemns images and leaves no doubt concerning the matter.

Yet, we do have an icon, but not one that we have made or

invented. There is one icon that is to be the object and the focus of our worship, the icon that is Jesus Christ. As we read from Colossians, "He is the image of the invisible God, the firstborn of all creation. For by him all things were created, in heaven and on earth, visible and invisible, whether thrones or dominions or rulers or authorities—all things were created through him and for him" (Colossians 1:15–16). And thus Christ is in the second commandment. And thus Christ fulfills the second commandment, because He, the image of the invisible God, is the icon whom we ponder.

Yet even as the icon, Jesus Christ is not a *visual* image for us—He is so much more than that. And thus this commandment is also for us, lest we turn our worship of Christ into another form of idolatry. We preach Christ crucified. We point to Christ in His glory. We preach the cross. We teach and preach all the things concerning the Christ. And we use *words*.

These words are given to us by God, Paul reminded us, in order that we would be instructed and encouraged. The second commandment is a clear condemnation of idols and images. We are not to use our creativity in order to fabricate an idol or to worship an image. We are called to know and love the God who made us for His glory. And that is the highest privilege any human being can know.

$\mathcal{The}$ THIRD COMMANDMENT

You shall not take the name of the Lord your God in vain, for the Lord will not hold him guiltless who takes his name in vain.

$\sim$ Exodus 20:7

3

Honoring the God
We Know by Name

Some years ago, the Federal Communications Commission created a list of seven bad words that were not to be spoken over the airwaves. My mother, like all moms I know, also kept a list of forbidden words. Her list was much, much larger than that of the FCC. I also was taught the little song:

> Be careful little lips what you say,
> Be careful little lips what you say.
> There is a Father up above
> Who's looking down in love,
> So be careful little lips what you say.[1]

When little lips were not careful with what they said, retribution was swift and punishment was sure. At the very least, this was an introduction to the power of words. How could a word—any word—create such a swift response? But words are far more powerful than they seem. Words are among the most powerful of the potent tools at our finite disposal.

In Exodus 20, in the first table of the law, we encounter the third commandment: "You shall not take the name of the Lord your God in vain, for the Lord will not hold him guiltless who takes his name in vain" (Exodus 20:7). Unfortunately, our apprehension of this commandment is generally far too simplistic and superficial. We assume if we can just avoid speaking the words on some list, we will do well. If, like the Federal Communications Commission, we can create our own list, publish it, distribute it, and remember it, all will be well. We know that in this world, words will be hurled with venom and blasphemy and with very little concern for the power of the word itself. Avoid such words, avoid "bad language," and we are safe.

Yet this commandment is regularly broken by many Christians. We violate this commandment in our conversation, in our piety, and in our worship.

SPEAKING HIS NAME WITH RESPECT

As we are seeing with each commandment, there is a covenantal context that we must take into account. Israel receives this treaty from the Lord in the form of these two tables of the law. Israel must stand out as this chosen and peculiar people from all the peoples of the world by their speech about God. After declaring that He will have no idols, God declares that His name must be spoken and heard with reverence.

Israel had come to know the God who brought the people out of bondage to Pharaoh in Egypt. This was the God who revealed Himself to Moses in an act of His grace and mercy. God disclosed Himself, forfeiting His personal privacy in the theophany of the bush that burned but was not consumed, in order that Moses would speak to the people, "I have heard from the Lord and this is His name."

This God revealed to Moses is not a generic deity of Middle Eastern piety and invention. This is the one true and living God. "I AM WHO I AM" (Exodus 3:14). The name declares God's own infinite perfection, His self-sufficiency, and His self existence. Idols are created things, something that exists because we have decided that it should be. But God names Himself "I AM WHO I AM." *I am* implies sovereignty and self-existence and all that is involved in the infinity of God's own perfections.

This is a revealed name. Flesh and blood did not reveal this name unto us, but our Father who is in heaven. It is a name about which God Himself is jealous. He just told us that He is jealous God: "For I the Lord your God am a jealous God, visiting the iniquity of the fathers on the children to the third and the fourth generation of those who hate me, but showing steadfast love to thousands of those who love me and keep my commandments" (20:5–6).

As you search the Scripture, you come to understand how God continued to reveal Himself through His names, revealing Himself as Provider, Healer, the Savior of Israel, the Almighty One, and many other names. These are not names of human invention or human discovery. "I AM WHO I AM"—this is God's revealed name to us. And in giving to us His name, the Father has given Himself to us. He has allowed His name to be known and spoken and even manipulated and maligned by sinful creatures. The Lord God is filled with zeal and jealousy for His name. In Ezekiel 36, the Lord God insists that He will rescue Israel for the sake of His own name:

> Therefore say to the house of Israel, Thus says the Lord God: It is not for your sake, O house of Israel, that I am about to act, but for the sake of my holy name, which you have profaned among the nations to which you came. And I will vindicate the holiness of my great name, which has been profaned among the nations, and which you have profaned among them. And the nations will know that I am the Lord, declares the Lord God, when through you I vindicate my holiness before their eyes. (Ezekiel 36:22–23)

Israel's serial disobedience is a sin against the holiness of God. Israel's weakness and the punishment that fell upon it is a blight upon the name of God, and God will not allow this to stand. It is not for

Israel's sake that He will act, but for the sake of His own name. It is not because of Israel that God will bring salvation, restoration, and the promise of a new covenant, but it is because of His name and His zeal for His own name. God will rescue Israel in order to defend His own reputation.

The church of the Lord Jesus Christ needs to hear that message today. It is not because of who we are that the church will endure, or the gospel will go forth. We do not secure God's promises—He does. He will not allow His name to be blasphemed among the nations without vindication. God's zeal for His own name explains the righteousness of His actions, and the absolute consistency of what He does for the glory of His own name.

So, what if the Third Commandment is not as simple as we thought it was? Maybe there is hidden danger here, one that would endanger our very souls and put at stake the very reputation of God—a reputation that He will vindicate. What if the Third Commandment extends to the totality of our faith? What if it extends to all that we would seek to do or to say or to think or to sing in worship? What if it extends to the far reaches of our discipleship? I want to suggest several ways we violate the Third Commandment, and several ways in which the contemporary church takes God's name in vain.

WE PROFANE GOD'S NAME
THROUGH REDUCTIONISTIC THEOLOGY

The first way we take God's name in vain is through reductionistic theology. To understand the name of God is to understand the power of the name, and the name implies an entire theology. The revelation of the name of God is a revelation of His character, perfections, sovereignty, power, holiness, and His love—and all these attributes are maligned, distorted, and denied in the reductionistic theologies rampant in our day.

God's name is taken in vain among theologians as a matter of routine practice. As a matter of fact, there are entire libraries of vanity where God's name is taken in vain. God has the sole right to define and to name Himself, and it is an act of creaturely arrogance and defiance to deny any component of His revealed name—or to seek to redefine it in a way that would make His character or His being more palatable for a postmodern age.

The Third Commandment follows fast on the second. God tells His people that not only does He forbid them to bring in an idol to worship, but that they must also not take His name in vain. To do so is to treat God as an idol and to impugn His reputation. To malign God's name is to misrepresent Him and thus to bear false witness to Him. We have no right to redefine God, but this is exactly what we do when we take His name in vain.

Theologians who reduce the power and perfections of God rob Him of His glory.

Reductionistic theologies are disguised forms of idolatry that in their false witness to God take His name in vain. These theologians who reduce the power and perfections of God rob Him of His glory. Here, Augustine again reminds us that there are only two loves—love of God and love of self—and everything tends toward one of these poles of love and affection.[2]

Reductionistic theologies are thus disguised forms of human self-love. They make God accountable to us, to our worldviews and our ideologies. In some sense, it was a lot easier to deal with the paganisms of old, for they were more honest forms of idolatry. We face now the persistent temptation to redefine God in our image, and to make of God an idol by the corruption of His name. We bring in wrong ideas about God, wrong teachings about His character, and we create an ideological idol in our own midst.

Although reductionistic theologies have been perennial in the church, many have arisen in the wake of the Enlightenment. Placing human wisdom, reason, and rationality at the very center of the universe, all things were brought under the reach and the accountability of human reason. Thus, the very *unreasonableness* of Jehovah, according to contemporary standards of rationality, is simply not to be accepted. These standards of rationality have nothing to do with the right operation of reason, but have everything to do with what we consider to be reasonable. They would have us believe it is not reasonable to speak of God and all of His perfections, His absolute sovereignty, or His omniscience—defined as His knowing all things.

The reductionistic theologies have everything to do with Christology, the doctrine of the Trinity, theology proper, and the doctrine of God. Desiring to cut God down to size, these theologies seek to accommodate the God of the Bible to contemporary standards of thought. As a result, in much of contemporary theology, we discover a desiccated, dehydrated, and demythologized deity—a God who bears no resemblance to Jehovah.

These reductionistic theologies cut God down to size. God's omniscience is declared to be limited, and God's intervention in history and the natural world are denied. Supernaturalism gives way to naturalism and God is redefined by those who would claim only to make God more "relevant" to our postmodern age.

Reductionistic theologies say that God must be accountable to our modern worldviews in such a way that we will make ourselves comfortable with Him. Modern and postmodern people are discomfited to know that God knows their very thoughts even before they think them, that God knows their deci-

> *In* much of contemporary theology, we discover a dehydrated and demythologized deity who bears no resemblance to Jehovah.

sions even before they make them. And yet, God is omniscient.

These various reductionisms are new and old, ranging from process theology to the language game of our contemporary day. You also see it in radical form, in the scandal of someone like John Shelby Spong, who is running out of material because there are no doctrines left to deny. It is also seen far more insidiously among those who consider themselves to be the faithful, but who nonetheless hold to understandings of God that are also dehydrated and demythologized, but more tamely so. There are far too many believers who think of God as being powerful and wise, but they never really understand what it means for Him to be omnipotent and omniscient.

In one sense, we have to give at least the old heretics their due for being honest and forthright in their heresies. Think of someone like Nietzsche, who said this:

> The Christian concept of a god—the god as the patron of the sick, the god as spinner of the cobwebs, the god as a spirit—is one of the most corrupt concepts that has ever been set up in the world: it probably touches the low watermark in the ebbing evolution of the god type.[3]

At least Nietzsche knew what he was rejecting. There once was a day when it took some real courage and conviction to deny God. But this dehydrated deity of popular piety requires no courage to deny. We have fallen from Nietzsche to Shirley MacLaine, and it is to our shame.

WE PROFANE GOD'S NAME
THROUGH TRIUMPHALISTIC PIETY

Second, we take the Lord's name in vain by our triumphalistic piety. If we could only hear ourselves talk—such chattering of religious nonsense! Just listen to our talk about God, or for that matter, read our bumper stickers: God is our co-pilot. Our dream weaver. Our life artist. Our friend. Our coach. Our therapist.

Not Jehovah! He renders no therapy. He offers no coaching. He weaves no dreams. He reveals Himself and saves His people from their sin. He rules over all the earth and no one can limit His power. The triviality and the triteness of our triumphalistic piety, the backslapping easy familiarity with the things of God and His own name—this is truly a scandal among us. We avoid a canon of forbidden words yet take the Lord's name in vain by the sheer triteness and cheapness of so much of how we speak when talking about God.

"God told me," "God showed me," and "God led me" are commonly used expressions of evangelical piety. Well, God does show, God does tell, and God does lead—by His revealed Word. Forms of disguised idolatry come among us when without any revealed, canonical, Scriptural word, we speak as if God has spoken to us and has given us a new revelation.

To our shame, a recent cover story in a national news magazine focused on prosperity theology—the kind of theology that promises health and wealth to all believers.[4] Well, God does want us rich, in the knowledge of His name and the experience of His glory. Prosperity theology did not emerge out of a vacuum, nor could it have emerged and taken hold if there had been a scriptural check upon the language that was spoken, the claims that were made, and the discourse of conversation about God. All this is to our shame because of the overfamiliarity of our language.

Prosperity theology is just one ugly example of what overfamiliarity looks like. In its least blatant form, the prosperity gospel still assures us that God wants us happy and fertile and well, overcoming our codependencies and living lives of authenticity—well-educated, safe, full, and satisfied.

All this triumphalistic piety comes upon us because we take the name of the Lord in vain. In reality, maybe the Lord actually wants us satisfied in Him and dissatisfied in everything else. Maybe God wants us to hunger and thirst for the glory of His name, and thus to risk physical hunger in order to be reminded of spiritual hunger. God would have us to thirst for righteousness when we often do not thirst at all.

WE PROFANE GOD'S NAME
THROUGH SUPERFICIAL WORSHIP

Third, we take the Lord's name in vain by superficial worship. God takes worship seriously, as demonstrated by the folly of Nadab and Abihu, who brought strange fire to the altar and were consumed by fire for the glory of God's own name (see Leviticus 10:1–3). In speaking to the woman at the well, Jesus proclaimed that the Father seeks those who will worship Him in spirit and in truth—never the one without the other (John 4:23). This is the glory of worship that is Word-centered, biblically regulated, scripturally established, Christ-focused, and Trinitarian. And yet, evangelicals turn worship into a laboratory of frivolities and a circus of creativities.

A half-century ago, A.W. Tozer spoke of worship, calling it the "missing jewel among evangelicals."[5] And Tozer spoke of those he described as the "joy bell boys," who pop out on the stage to be seen— and now, of course, on popular television as well.[6] The joy bell boys are among us. We are told that worship must be fun, worship must be creative. And all idolatrous worship *is* fun and creative, not necessarily fun in the sense of frivolity (just ask the prophets of Baal in 1 Kings 18), but in the sense of being narcissistic and self-focused.

The horizon of our worship is simply too low. We welcome God to our services as if He is a guest. We take the Lord's name in vain in our superficial worship and our worship betrays us, demonstrating what we genuinely believe. When we worship, our prayers, sermons, and songs all reveal what we genuinely believe. We should be required to listen to ourselves.

This is not a broadside against contemporary music. Frankly, much of it is better than the music it replaced. I am generationally chastised and warned against making broadside attacks. John Piper is right when he says that a generation raised on "Do Lord, O Do Lord, O Do Remember Me," is not well positioned to criticize the young. However, I do have firsthand anecdotal knowledge of what has to be the absolute lowest form of a so-called worship song. It was not difficult to memorize this atrocity, for it contains only a few words. The only pleasure

I could take in the song was seeing my teenage children look at me with the recognition of how awful it was. I had to look it up on the Internet to believe that it actually existed. Its key line: "I'll do my best. I'll do my best, Jesus . . . for you." Basically those words were repeated throughout the song, with an "Oo, Oo, Oo" thrown in the middle.

The song was capped off by the worship leader at the end saying, "That is just the way it is, isn't it? God just wants us to do our best!"

Where was Samson to bring down the pillars of the temple on the idol worshipers? *Just do your best?* God never reduces the gospel to anything remotely like this.

Our superficial worship betrays us in the worst ways. God takes His name seriously, but we often do not—not if we think this is merely a matter of style. Although the Bible offers no revealed musical taste, there is a revealed name, and there is a necessary reverence and dignity attached to that name. There is danger attached to that name, just as there is a danger represented in the attempt to change the language of worship about God—including feminist God language and all the rest. We dare not slander God by taking His name in vain in our worship. Once again, the real issue is idolatry. To take God's name in vain is to fabricate a new God.

WE PROFANE GOD'S NAME
THROUGH MANIPULATIVE GOD-TALK

Fourth, we break this command to not take God's name in vain by our manipulative God-talk. Well-known Yale law professor Stephen Carter wrote,

In truth, there is probably no country in the Western world where people use God's name quite as much or quite as publicly or for quite as many purposes as we Americans do. The third commandment not withstanding, few candidates for office are able to end their speeches without asking God to bless their audience or the nation or the great work we're undertaking. Everybody is sure that the other side is sincere. Athletes thank God on television after scoring the winning touchdown. Politicians like to thank God as on their side.[7]

The challenge here is deeply theological. We have no right to speak where God has not spoken. You see, it is not just the misuse of God's name by a politician that troubles me. I am far more concerned with the misuse of God's name by Christians, pastors, public figures, church members, where we would dare speak where God has not spoken. We would dare to speak as if we were speaking in His name and speaking in His stead. The Lord's name is taken in vain when we say things like, "We know why God did that," or "I can tell you why you have cancer," or "I can explain to the nation why Hurricane Katrina hit New Orleans." God's name is taken in vain.

Turn on the television and you will find many who follow the example of Eliphaz the Temanite, the friend of Job who shows up to explain why God did this or God did that or what God is saying to us in this or that. These TV Eliphazes often speak where God has not spoken, where God has not given them license to explain His ways. As the apostle Paul asks: "For who has known the mind of the Lord, or who has been his counselor? Or who has given a gift to him that he might be repaid?" (Romans 11:34–35) God's ways are past finding out.

The tongue betrays and reveals the heart. The Third Commandment has everything to do with our worship.

The Third Commandment contains a clear threat that "the Lord will not hold him guiltless who takes his name in vain." Not guiltless! So there is guilt among us, and there is guilt around us. The Lord takes His name with such seriousness that He will vindicate His name, among the nations and among the name-breakers.

So, does this commandment have application to the taking of oaths by Christians? Of course it does. Does it have to do with profanity? Yes, of course, that is included too. There are many biblical principles concerning the importance of speech and the danger of the tongue. Does this command warn us against the misuse of the divine name? Yes. Is there a list of forbidden words? Yes there is, and you don't have to have a degree in linguistics to understand why. The tongue betrays and reveals the heart. The Third Commandment has everything to do with our worship, with the disposition of our heart, and with our knowledge or ignorance of the one true and living God. The command reaches to the depths of our discipleship, and it extends to everything we touch and everything we think that is even remotely theological or spiritual. It extends to our marriages, to our parenting, and to the totality of our lives, because God makes total claim upon us by His name. John Calvin, in preaching on this very commandment, gets it exactly right:

> The purpose of this commandment is—God wills that we hallow the majesty of His name. Therefore it means, in brief, that we are not to profane His name by treating it contemptuously and irreverently. To this prohibition duly corresponds the commandment that we should be zealous and careful to honor His name with godly reverence. Therefore, we ought to be so disposed in mind and speech that we neither think nor say anything concerning God and His mysteries without reverence and with much soberness, that in estimating His works we conceive nothing but what is honorable to Him.[8]

As we look to the new covenant in Christ, we recognize that not only is this command fulfilled in Christ, but the commandment will be universally and consciously fulfilled upon His return. We move from Exodus 20 to Philippians 2 and understand a day shall come when "every tongue [will] confess that Jesus Christ is Lord, to the glory of God the Father" (verse 11). And when that name is understood, all will be well, and all will be answered, and all will be right.

The eschatological fulfillment of that promise is what brings us to true Christian worship as we invoke the name of God with reverence and with awe and with fear, and as we look to that day when God will vindicate His name among the nations. He will do so in that name which He has given, that name which He has revealed—the name of His Son, even Jesus Christ our Lord. The name of Jesus will vindicate the name of the Father as the Father vindicates the name of the Son.

So how shall we live in light of this commandment? I suppose that the children's Sunday school verse still rings true:

> *Be careful little lips what you say,*
> *Be careful little lips what you say.*
> *There is a Father up above*
> *Who's looking down in love,*
> *So be careful little lips what you say.*

The FOURTH COMMANDMENT

Remember the Sabbath day, to keep it holy. Six days you shall labor, and do all your work, but the seventh day is a Sabbath to the Lord your God. On it you shall not do any work, you, or your son, or your daughter, your male servant, or your female servant, or your livestock, or the sojourner who is within your gates. For in six days the Lord made heaven and earth, the sea, and all that is in them, and rested the seventh day. Therefore the Lord blessed the Sabbath day and made it holy.

～ Exodus 20:8–11

4

Resting Secure in the God Who Saves Us

When young, life is a matter of rather simple dos and don'ts. There are two tablets of action, two tables of morality—the permitted and the forbidden.

On the one table, the dos: obey parents, walk silently in line to class, sit still, eat your vegetables, be nice to your sister. On the other table: do not run into the street, stick not thy finger into the electrical outlet, do not pull your sister's hair, do not pull the dog's tail, do not make fun of your teacher. These tables are clearly understood, formally delineated, strictly applied, and consistently reinforced.

Those *were* days of moral clarity. But there comes a day when one understands there is a reason behind all of these dos and don'ts. There is not only the functionality of a moral etiquette; there is the theology of a moral urgency.

A TIME OF MORAL AMBIGUITY

I can remember one of my first times experiencing acute moral ambiguity. It occurred in relation to Sunday afternoon and my car. I was sixteen years old, and I had my first car. It was a mean machine. A 1964 Ford Fairlane—black paint, red vinyl interior, an air conditioner that didn't work but looked good hanging from underneath the dash. This Fairlane was the object of my almost complete fascination.

One Sunday afternoon, as I washed my car—an act of spiritual devotion to the car—my mother observed this and went into a "mother moment." Every sixteen-year-old boy knows what this looks like. Mom came out of the house with a look of absolute moral, theological, almost divine indignation upon her face.

"What are you doing?"

"I'm washing my car."

"Don't you know it is Sunday?" she asked. In fact, I did know it was Sunday.

"You are breaking the Sabbath command," she continued.

To be honest, given my idolatrous love affair with my car, it was the second command, not the fourth that I was in such great danger of breaking. I remember standing there with a half-washed car, half soaped and half not, and wondering what in the world I had done to deserve this matriarchal moral onslaught. More than that, what in the world was behind all this? How was I supposed to know now what was on the "do" and "do not do" list?

Washing one's own car was fairly restful, seemed rather urgent, and was even merciful, loosely speaking. I knew there must be more to thinking it through than this. However, the car remained half-washed and half-unwashed—and this was because I was to honor my mother.

FIGURING OUT THE SABBATH

So, how are we to understand the Fourth Commandment? My own Sabbath crisis was not based in any detailed theology, just the personal experience of washing a car. I knew that my mother's outrage had to do not only with the car and the water and the suds and the sun, but that it also concerned the neighbors. What would the neighbors think? Evidently, the Sabbath implied acts that were not to be done on Sunday. I never had a clear list.

Literature is replete with references to Sunday as the day on which there can be no fun. And for some Christians, it almost seems as if that is the defining factor. If you enjoy doing it, then you probably are not supposed to be doing it on Sunday. However, if you do not enjoy doing it, then this is probably the day for it.

And that in itself portrays something of the sick-souled nature of much of our concern about Sunday, the Lord's Day. The early Christians *yearned* to arrive at the Lord's Day, knowing that if only they could survive the week, they would once again hear the preaching of the Word of God and fellowship with the saints of God. They thought, "If we can only survive the week, we will make it to the Lord's Day together."

IS THERE A SABBATH PATTERN FOR US?

In contrast to contemporary confusion, there is abundant clarity in the Old Testament regarding the purpose of the Sabbath for Israel. The covenantal context of this passage explains the central role the Sabbath would play in the life of God's chosen people, Israel. The Sabbath would be an institutional, public, and absolutely obvious indication of Israel's special status as Yahweh's people. He is a holy God who makes claim upon the totality of the life of His people—their calendar, their time, and their Sabbath day. All these served as an expression of their status as God's people. The Lord lays claim over all things and all moments and all days, but He made a special claim upon this day for His covenant people.

Within the command, there is an explicit reference to Genesis 2:1–3:

Thus the heavens and the earth were finished, and all the host of them. And on the seventh day God finished his work that he had done, and he rested on the seventh day from all his work that he had done. So God blessed the seventh day and made it holy, because on it God rested from all his work that he had done in creation.

From this text, we understand that creation itself offers a Sabbath pattern that we may have not detected earlier. This leads us to think through one of the first and most difficult questions we encounter regarding the Sabbath: Is this a universal command for all humanity? Is the command written into the natural order of things, such that the unsinful eye should have recognized it, or is honoring the Sabbath a special command that is part of the Mosaic covenant for Israel and Israel alone?

Geerhardus Vos argued that the command is in creation itself, as evidenced by Genesis 2, and that the Sabbath is to be a pattern of moral law for all peoples and all times everywhere—six days of labor, one day of rest.[1] If a convincing case for that argument can be made, then Vos makes it.

I must admit, though, that I am unconvinced. For one thing, there is no universal recognition among peoples around the world of a Sabbath pattern. There is not even a universal acceptance or recognition among peoples throughout history of a seven-day week. If it is written into the law of nature, then it was not obvious even to the ancient Hebrews. Vestiges of all the other commandments are found in the natural order of things, as God revealed Himself as Creator in that natural order. But the law written on the human heart does not universally indicate knowledge of the Sabbath.

Furthermore, in the experience of Israel, the Sabbath as a day of rest on the seventh day emerges only in the Mosaic period, the period of the Exodus. During the story of Israel's wilderness wanderings, we read that on the Sabbath day an Israelite would not gather manna in the wilderness. Rather, a double portion had to be gathered on the sixth day in order that there would be food on the seventh. However, by the time we come to Exodus 20, the giving of the Ten Commandments, the verb that is first used for the Sabbath is the verb *remember*. So it would seem by this point, and certainly evidenced by the gathering of manna, that there was some understanding of a Sabbath pattern: "Six days you shall labor, and do all your work, but the seventh day is a Sabbath to the Lord your God (verses 9–10)."

The worldview of the Ten Commandments honors labor. We are commissioned and commanded to work. In the curse given after the fall, we are told that it is by the sweat of man's brow that the earth will yield forth its fruit (Genesis 3:17–19). And yet, although labor is dignified throughout the Scripture, labor is only a temporary reality that passes quickly. All that man does so quickly turns to dust.

Human labor is dignified, but it is also put in its place.

The Sabbath was a rest unto the Lord, and He linked it to His own work in creation. Israel's Sabbath pointed backwards to God's Sabbath during the week of creation, even as it also points forward in time to something that will be an even greater fulfillment than rest on this day. Even as circumcision was to be the mark of entrance into the covenant, so also the Sabbath observance marked Israel as God's people. And it was not only for those who were children of the covenant, but for all those who were in the nation. Take note in both Exodus and Deuteronomy how the command is extended to others: "The seventh day is a Sabbath to the Lord your God. On it you shall not do any work, you, or your son, or your daughter, your male servant, or your female servant, or your livestock, or the sojourner who is within your gates" (Exodus 20:10).

Even the livestock observed the Sabbath! This is to be a day that is holy, set apart unto the Lord, for the Lord Himself is holy. Human labor is dignified, but it is also put in its place.

In Nehemiah, we read a famous passage dealing with Israel's rebellion and failure concerning the Sabbath:

In those days I saw in Judah people treading winepresses on the Sabbath, and bringing in heaps of grain and loading them on donkeys and also wine, grapes, figs, and all kinds of loads, which they brought into Jerusalem on the Sabbath day. And I warned them on the day when they sold food. Tyrians also, who lived in the city, brought in fish and all kinds of goods and sold them on the Sabbath to the people of Judah, in Jerusalem itself! Then I confronted the nobles of Judah and said to them, "What is this evil thing that you are doing, profaning the Sabbath day? Did not your fathers act in this way, and did not our God bring all this disaster on us and on this city? Now you are bringing more wrath on Israel by profaning the Sabbath." (Nehemiah 13:15–18)

Looking both backward and to the present, Nehemiah focused on the sin of breaking the Sabbath, knowing that God will bring judgment upon the people for disobedience. The very nature of their present exile could be partly explained in terms of their past Sabbath breaking. Nehemiah went on to say:

As soon as it began to grow dark at the gates of Jerusalem before the Sabbath, I commanded that the doors should be shut and gave orders that they should not be opened until after the Sabbath. And I stationed some of my servants at the gates, that no load might be brought in on the Sabbath day. Then the merchants and sellers of all kinds of wares lodged outside Jerusalem once or twice. But I warned them and said to them, "Why do you lodge outside the wall? If you do so again, I will lay hands on you." From that time on they did not come on the Sabbath. Then I commanded the Levites that they should purify themselves and come and guard the gates, to keep the Sabbath day holy. (13:19–22a)

This is serious Sabbath keeping, a high fence around the day. This is a direct link, a connection between the security and safety of the nation and the profaning of the Sabbath. Thus, we see the fourth commandment in both its explicit statement and also in terms of Israel's experience.

THE COMMAND FULFILLED BY
THE LORD OF THE SABBATH

As we come to the New Testament, particularly in the gospels, the centrality of the Sabbath institution within Judaism becomes very clear. And yet, we also understand that something new is added to the Sabbath. The Sabbath in the Old Testament had been primarily a day of rest. Although Leviticus refers to a "holy convocation" on the Sabbath, it is clear that the Sabbath is primarily a day of rest, not a day of worship. Then, in the rise of the synagogue, Israel had opportunity to gather together, as depicted in passages where Jesus spent time reading the Scriptures in the synagogues on the Sabbath day. And yet, even as Jesus observed the Sabbath, He declared that He Himself is the fulfillment of the Sabbath. It is not that He will obey the Sabbath command; it is that He will indeed represent and fulfill the Sabbath command, for He is Lord of the Sabbath.

In a famous contest with the Pharisees, when His disciples are accused of breaking the Sabbath because they gathered wheat as they walked through a field, Jesus said, in paraphrase, "If you want to catch them in a misdemeanor, I will give you a felony. I am Lord of the Sabbath. You will not interpret the Sabbath to me. I will interpret the Sabbath for all" (Matthew 12:7–8).

Jesus honored and recognized the Sabbath, but even more importantly, He identified Himself as the Lord of the Sabbath. As the Lord of the Sabbath, He established that the Sabbath was made for man, not man for the Sabbath.

If an egg is found under a hen on the Sabbath morning, may it be eaten? When, after all, is the labor performed?

The Pharisees become Exhibit A of what happens when

Sabbath keeping is turned into theological casuistry. By the first century, Jewish rabbis gave intense attention to debating Sabbath restrictions. My favorite such debate is this: If an egg is found under a hen on the Sabbath morning, may it be eaten? It is a technical question. When, after all, is the labor performed? The hen is not available for interrogation. If the egg was the product of labor on the Sabbath, it is not to be eaten. If, however, the labor was done on some other day and it just appears on the Sabbath, then it is a gift. What kind of casuistry is this? Which egg can you scramble, and which must you destroy?

A tragic missing of the point lay at the heart of much of Israel's experience by the time Jesus entered the earthly scene. Another such question: What if the elderly woman of the family, the matriarch, should fall in the field and needed to be brought back to the house? Could you take a litter to her in order to bring her out of the field? The rabbis debated this back and forth, some saying yes and some saying no. Some said no because it was too dangerous, for in taking out the wooden stakes, the poles that would be a part of the litter might drop and dig a furrow in the ground, and one would have plowed and desecrated the Sabbath. Was it better to leave Granny in the field than to desecrate the Sabbath by plowing? This is the kind of logic that Jesus would not abide.

One Sabbath day, the Pharisees thought they had Jesus right where they wanted Him as they presented to Him a man with a withered hand. They asked, "Is it lawful to heal on the Sabbath?" (Matthew 12:10).

Jesus answered them with a question. "Which one of you who has a sheep, if it falls into a pit on the Sabbath, will not take hold of it and lift it out? Of how much more value is a man than a sheep! So it is lawful to do good on the Sabbath" (verses 11–12).

Then He said to the man, "Stretch out your hand" (verse 13). Jesus demonstrated that He was Lord of the Sabbath even before He spoke as Lord of the Sabbath. "Stretch out your hand," He said, and it was restored just as the other.

Earlier that same day, Jesus had rebuked the Pharisees, who often served as the religious traffic cops, waiting and wanting to write tickets about Sabbath breaking. They thought they had caught Jesus' disciples in an infringement, an infraction of the Sabbath. Jesus responded, in effect, "It would be helpful if you boys had read the Bible. You would have read that even on the Sabbath the priests work. You would know that even David and his men went inside and took the holy bread which was not for them but they ate it and they did not die. I am Lord of the Sabbath!"(see Matthew 12:3–9).

The first-century context is one of Sabbath confusion and Sabbath corruption.

The first-century context is one of Sabbath confusion and Sabbath corruption, so that instead of seeing the Sabbath as made for man, man was understood to be made for the Sabbath. It became both an imposition and a mere institution. But God alone has the right to define the Sabbath, and He ultimately does so in Christ.

THE SABBATH REPLACED BY RESURRECTION SUNDAY

But what about the church? When we look to the experience of the church, in the book of Acts and the remainder of the New Testament, we do not find a Sabbatarian pattern. We do not find an observance of the Jewish Sabbath. Instead, we find the celebration of the Lord's Day. This was an issue of some controversy, something reflected in the very text of the New Testament. When we come to Acts 20:7, we see the believers gathered on the first day of the week, explicitly tying the first day of the week with the resurrection of Jesus Christ from the dead.

The Lord of the Sabbath was raised from the dead not on the Sabbath day but on the first day of the week, thus redefining our calendar and putting this first day at the center of our week. Observance and commemoration and celebration of the resurrection of Christ become the calendar issue for us in a seven-day pattern. This is repeated in other places, implicit and explicit in the New Testament.

It is on the first day of the week that Paul commands that the Corinthians take a collection for the church in Jerusalem (1 Corinthians 16:1–2), implying that Sunday is the day on which they gathered together. In the story of infamous Eutychus—known for falling asleep and falling out a window during a sermon—Paul stretched himself upon Eutychus and the boy was brought back to life, demonstrating the power of God (Acts 20:7–12). From the context of the Acts passage, it appears these Christians had been doing on the Lord's Day what they would have done any other day of the week—working—except that they are gathered for worship at the end of the day. In the imperial economy of Rome, the concept of a "weekend" had not yet been imagined, so there were no days set apart for leisure without work. We always tend to read the Scriptures by our contemporary experience, without recognizing the different cultural context in which they were written. The invention of the weekend is a relatively recent and almost entirely Western reality, explainable in the history of our civilization, but certainly not universal.

ENTERING INTO A SABBATH REST

Within the church, Sabbath keeping has became something of a controversy. However, the most important issue for us is that the Sabbath has been fulfilled in Christ. In Psalm 95, God Himself warns that those who will not hear and heed His Word will not enter into His rest. The Old Testament points to a rest that is beyond the seventh-day rest. There is a rest for which Israel is to yearn and is to long—a rest to be fulfilled in the consolation of Israel.

This is messianic, finding complete fulfillment in Christ. Hebrews 4:9–10 says: "So then, there remains a Sabbath rest for the people of God, for whoever has entered God's rest has also rested from his works as God did from his." The writer of Hebrews speaks of a promised Sabbath rest that is a rest of salvation—both present experience and eschatological expectation. This rest is accomplished by the atonement of the Lord Jesus Christ, perfectly accomplished for us as He paid in full the penalty for our sins.

Thus, the most important issue of Sabbath rest in the New Testament is that we rest *in* Christ and we rest *from* our labors—from all efforts to be saved by our works. We cannot work for our salvation. We may only rest in Christ, and in Christ we find a total rest. We cease from our labors to save ourselves. We rest from our works as God did from His. The concern of the writer of Hebrews is the hardness of our heart, a refusal to hear and to obey, which would become the reason why souls will not enter the Sabbath rest. The Sabbath is fulfilled in Christ, and is tied to belief (Hebrews 3:19). There is the promise of entering this rest, and we are told to rest from our works as God did from His. This is a breathtakingly beautiful portrait of our salvation. We are justified by faith, not by works.

OPTION I: OBSERVE THE SABBATH ON THE SEVENTH DAY

So what is the relationship between the Fourth Commandment and the Christian church? There are only three main options to consider. The first is *seventh-day Sabbatarianism*, teaching that the Fourth Commandment continues unaltered in the life of the Christian church, as it had existed for the nation of Israel. Thus, there is a seventh-day Sabbatarianism that is almost completely consistent in its logic, and I would argue almost certainly wrong according to the biblical text. They may ask you why it is that you are a Sabbath breaker, and why it is that you worship on Sunday.

Advocates of the seventh-day Sabbath should be given the tribute of their consistency. Yet this view often falls into a legalism. More importantly, it flies in the face of New Testament practice and teaching, wherein we find the new covenant people together on the first day of the week, not the seventh. Christians gathered on the first day of the week, not on the Jewish Sabbath. Paul's missiological strategy was to go into the synagogues on the Sabbath and to preach Christ to the gathered Jews. But the church itself gathered on the Lord's Day, the first day of the week.

There is no New Testament mention whatsoever of seventh-day

practice in the church. Passages like Romans 14 and Colossians 2 tell us that this is not to be an issue among Christians:

> Therefore let no one pass judgment on you, in questions of food and drink, or with regard to a festival or a new moon or a Sabbath. These are a shadow of the things to come, but the substance belongs to Christ. . . . If with Christ you died to the elemental spirits of the world, why, as if you were still alive in the world, do you submit to regulations—"Do not handle, Do not taste, Do not touch" (referring to things that all perish as they are used)—according to human precepts and teachings? These have indeed an appearance of wisdom in promoting self-made religion and asceticism and severity to the body, but they are of no value in stopping the indulgence of the flesh. (Colossians 2:16–17, 20–23)

Then, in Romans, we find a categorical statement. Paul makes clear in Romans 14 that it is perfectly fine for Jewish believers to continue to gather in the synagogue with other Jews on the Sabbath day. It is perfectly fine for them to be bound by their own traditions and by their own consciences in observing the Sabbath. But it is wrong to bind the conscience of the church in terms of this observance, and there is no reference to this observance in the New Testament.

OPTION 2: OBSERVE THE SABBATH
ON THE FIRST DAY

The second option is *Lord's Day Sabbatarianism*. It is understood that the church does indeed gather together rightly on the first day of the week rather than the seventh. Explicit in this position is a transfer theology that says the fourth commandment stipulation of the seventh day is transferred to the first day under the new covenant.

Again, there is logic to this position, and not only that, there is also a great theological tradition and heritage in this teaching. The Westminster Confession is the quintessential expression of this position, stating:

"This Sabbath is to be kept holy unto the Lord, when men, after a due preparing of their hearts, and ordering of their common affairs beforehand, do not only observe an holy rest all the day from their own works, words, and thoughts about their worldly employments and recreations, but also are taken up the whole time in the public and private exercises of His worship, and in the duties of necessity and mercy.[2]

The Westminster Confession makes clear claims that the Lord's Day is a Christian Sabbath. There has been a transfer, it explicitly claims, of the day from the seventh to the first. Again, although there is a consistent logic, there is no New Testament evidence that such an observance was practiced. There is simply no textual basis for this transfer, either in terms of an explicit passage that says that it has taken place according to the Lord's command, or in terms of the implicit reference to the practice of the early church in observing something that would reflect this transfer.

Is the Lord's Day a Christian Sabbath? There is no biblical text that makes this transfer.

The Sabbatarian tradition developed most especially in seventeenth-century English-speaking evangelicalism. During this time, a form of Sabbatarian thought had emerged as there arose the requirement of coming up with a rationale for why civil law should hold the first day to be special. The requirement of coming up with an argument for the civil law produced a form of Sabbatarianism, but it was the English Sabbatarians who quintessentially formalized the evangelical understanding of first-day, or Lord's Day, Sabbatarianism. This became the practice of the Puritans. The Lord's Day was treated as a universal Christian institution, Sabbatarian in its nature.

However, the key issue is this: is the Lord's Day a Christian Sabbath? The problem is that there is no text that makes this transfer, and there is, I would argue, no clear New Testament warrant whatsoever. Indeed, Paul seems adamant that this is not the case, in the texts we just examined (Romans 14 and Colossians 2).

Part of our confusion here has to do with the central purpose of the Lord's Day. Is it the same as the central purpose of the Sabbath? Is it mostly about rest? I would argue that it is not. The evidence in the New Testament is that the Lord's Day is mostly about worship, about gathering, about being confronted with the preaching of the Word, about coming together with mutual instruction, about the Lord's Table, where the communion of the saints points to a meal which is yet to come. The Lord's Day points not only back to the resurrection of the Lord Jesus Christ and His accomplished work, but it also points forward eschatologically to that rest we will enjoy on that day when we shall be with Him and there will be no more work. There will be no more evangelism. There will be no more missions. There will be no more works of mercy, no benevolent ministries in heaven, for there will be mercy in abundance. All will be well. Every eye will be dry and every tear will be wiped away.

The context of the Lord's Day is different than the context of the Sabbath, whereas the purpose of the Lord's Day is different than the purpose of the Sabbath.

OPTION 3: PARTICIPATE IN WORSHIP ON "THE LORD'S DAY"

The third main position is *Lord's Day observance*. This is the position of the Reformers, in particular of John Calvin and Martin Luther. It is the position of most evangelical Christians around the world. The central issue for the church is the command to gather together on the Lord's Day, not forsaking the assembling of themselves and fulfilling all that is commanded in the New Testament. All that we do in worship, from the preaching of the Word to the singing of psalms and hymns and spiritual songs, to the mutual edification of the body, to the fellowship that we enjoy in the observance of the Lord's Table that proclaims His life, His death, and His resurrection until He comes—all of this Lord's Day observance focuses on the positive content of the Lord's Day, and the positive expectation that God's people will yearn for this day. The main issue is what we are to *do*, rather than what we are *not to do* on the Lord's Day.

One problem with so much of our thinking about the Lord's Day is that it is natural for us to think of it as an imposition in our otherwise busy schedule. And yet we are to be faithful to gather together, making it a priority of our lives to be with God's people. And as we are with fellow believers, we gather together to prepare for eternity, to be confronted by the Word of God, to edify one another, and to yearn for that eternal rest that is promised to us by the grace and mercy of God.

ANOTHER OPTION: THE PRACTICE OF NONOBSERVANCE

You will notice that I mentioned three major options, each having its own consistency, each attempting to wrestle with the biblical text, and each attempting to understand the responsibility of the church. But there is a fourth option which is really no option at all, and this is *Lord's Day nonobservance.* And yet, throughout contemporary evangelicalism, this fourth option creeps its way into our practice. The Lord's Day is being marginalized, no longer treated as an institution of biblical significance and eschatological promise, instead being treated as something with which we may play. In many of our churches, we are now following a logic that betrays the Lord's Day by suggesting that if you will just come for this activity, you are then complete in terms of your responsibility for this day.

I think in my own lifetime of how this has changed. We woke up early in the morning on the Lord's Day, we put on special clothes. I can still remember, even in my youngest years, putting on giant white clunky leather shoes. I remember we had special clothes for Sunday we did not get to wear any other day of the week. It was the Lord's

Day. I can still remember the smell and the sound of the nursery in the church. I can still remember what it was like to go into big church for the first time—it seemed so huge that it would swallow us. I can remember sitting on the pew when my legs could not touch the ground, dangling with the heavy white leather, being told by insistence of word and of hand to stop wiggling.

We were there for Sunday school in the morning, and then we were there for morning worship, and after morning worship, we shared a family meal, often with the larger family and extended family. And then, almost as quickly as we had left, we were back for Training Union and choir practice and evening worship, and after that fellowship with God's people at the church.

It was an all-consuming day—and I am so thankful for it. I do not know who I would be if not for being with God's people on that day as much as I was, by God's grace and mercy in my life. I do not know who I would be today if I had not had such opportunity to be confronted with the Word of God, not only just in a service where the Word of God was declared, thanks be to God, but also in so many other opportunities of Bible study and Christian nurture and Christian experience with the saints.

As I am confronted by the Fourth Commandment, I am convicted not about Sabbath keeping, but about Lord's Day breaking. I am convicted that as I read the fourth commandment, that Israel's responsibility to keep the Sabbath was, if anything, less important and the church's responsibility to observe the Lord's Day more important. It is not mere ceremony. It is to be that day anticipated and longed for. It is not an imposition. It is to be our confidence that if we can only survive the week, if we can only arrive at the Lord's Day, we shall be with God's people together. We can survive imperial oppression. We can survive the drudgery of what appears to be meaningless labor. We can survive persecution and trial. We can endure sickness and death— if only we can arrive at the Lord's Day to be with God's people together.

How pale and tepid and weak, how compromising and conflicted appears our thought of the Lord's Day. I offer no tables or lists. It is not a Sabbath; it is the central Christian institution for our worship and gathering. It is distinct from other days; it is set apart for worship.

Are there things we ought not to do on the Lord's Day? Certainly there are. Anything that would detract from our worship should not be done on the Lord's Day. Anything that would rob the Lord's Day of priority worship should not be done. Anything that would be on our minds when we are worshiping, as if we can only get done with this in order to go do that, is a matter of sin, no matter what it is.

> *The* Lord's Day is not a Sabbath; it is the central Christian institution for our worship and gathering.

Was it a sin for me to wash my car on that Sunday afternoon? I still do not know. I do know this. I was a sinner on that day saved by the grace of God, who when he thought of the Lord's Day, had no real understanding of the rest that the Lord of the Sabbath had accomplished for me. I knew of salvation, but I did not know of that picture of our salvation, and I should have. I don't know if I would have washed my car or not, but I would have had a very different understanding of the Lord's Day.

Israel was called to obey the Fourth Commandment and to "observe the Sabbath." The church is called to find rest in Christ and to give ourselves to worship on the day that marks His resurrection from the dead. We cannot obey the fourth commandment if we do not understand the transformation of the Sabbath as it is fulfilled in Christ.

The FIFTH COMMANDMENT

Honor your father and your mother, that your days may be long in the land that the Lord your God is giving you.

~ Exodus 20:12

5

Honoring Our Parents, Cherishing a Patrimony

The fifth commandment teaches: "Honor your father and your mother, that your days may be prolonged." Or, as comedian Bill Cosby says, "I brought you into this world, and I can take you out."

We think we are familiar with this commandment because it has the ring of the familiar. Most of us have heard it like this since we were children: "Honor your father and your mother" equals "Obey Dad and Mom." That is the depth of our understanding of the commandment, and it *is* a correct understanding, though woefully incomplete.

We live in an age of intentional orphans. All around us are people who would disregard and disrespect their patrimony, who would reject the tradition and throw off all the inheritance of father and mother in order to be as orphans. The modern psychotherapeutic community tells us that we must kill off our parents if we are to be authentic selves and grow into true adulthood. Abraham Lincoln spoke to this when he told the parable of a man on trial for murdering his parents, who then threw himself on the mercy of the court, claiming that he was now an orphan. This generation is much like that, a generation that rejects its own patrimony and is marked by rebelliousness and rootlessness. It is a generation cut off from tradition, culture, wisdom, experience, and truth. It is inconceivable to the worldview of the Scripture that we would dishonor our father and mother and orphan ourselves.

But this current spirit is not an entirely new spirit. A spirit of disregard and disobedience, a spirit of rejection, a spirit of intentional orphanage—this is as old as the fall of Adam and Eve. But every generation devises new ways of disregarding its patrimony and new ways of overthrowing a precious inheritance and treasury.

Like the nine other commandments, the Fifth Commandment is set in the context of the covenantal history of Israel. As the people of the covenant, the children of Israel were promised a land. Canaan, the land of promise, was their inheritance from God. And yet, they were told that in order to be prolonged there, they must honor father and mother.

A COMMANDMENT FOR ADULTS

We are far too comfortable with this commandment because we think it is addressed to children. But this is not children's church in the middle of the Ten Commandments. It is not as if we have nine grown-up, adult commandments—dealing with things like adultery, murder, idolatry, and taking the Lord's name in vain—and then all of a sudden a commandment that is addressed to the children. God was not looking for a way to involve the children in this tenfold moral code. Obeying father and mother is certainly part of this commandment, but that is not the completeness of what this commandment means.

To the contrary, what we have here is a commandment addressed primarily to adults. To God's elect and chosen nation, this command comes in the midst of covenant. To honor the one true and living God is to honor father and mother. This commandment is not just about obeying mother and father lest we bear their wrath, and it is not merely to keep us from running out into the street or sticking paper clips in electrical outlets. It is about honoring father and mother, and receiving the patrimony. As God's people we are called to this commandment of honor, even as it is addressed to Israel.

As we have learned, the first table of the law deals with those commandments most specifically delineating the relationship between the Creator and His covenant people. But in the second table of the law, dealing with human relationships, God's people are to be characterized by certain behaviors that in their very essence point to Himself. This law that was given to Israel is not just a therapeutic device in order that Israel *might* have family happiness. As Professor Christopher Wright correctly notes, the fifth commandment forms part of the structure and fabric of Israel's relationship with God.[1] It is not merely a recipe for happy families. This is the command of a holy God whose people are to live this way in order to display His own character in their lives.

Faithfulness begins at home.

Covenantal faithfulness begins at home. Upon reflection, intuitively we know this to be true. If we fail to learn what covenantal faithfulness is at home, how can we understand it in a larger context?

The institution of the family presents us with an essential question in these postmodern times. Is the family a natural or a supernatural development? Is the family an accidental by-product of human social evolution or is it a supernatural gift given to us by the Creator for our good and for our holiness? If we believe the family is simply a by-product of human social evolution, then we can evolve beyond it. And we live in the midst of a postmodern age determined to evolve beyond it. But if the family is the gift of a holy God, then we are talking about more than a breeding couple and their privileged offspring. A covenantal relationship of marriage mirrors the character of God's relationship with His people. Thus, the children that are given to them as gifts are raised in a covenant household in order that they may also by their correct relationship between children and parents demonstrate the relationship between God and His own people.

It is often said and it is so clearly true that our relationship with our parents in terms of the most formative period of our lives will to a great degree indicate our relationship with God. We either come under the authority of our parents willingly, or we respond to that authority with a spirit of rebellion. Our response to our parents indicates how we will respond to our Creator.

HONORING THE PATRIARCHS

Within this covenant at Sinai, God told Israel of the behavior expected of His covenant people, and the structure and relation of God's covenant families. Covenant families demonstrate His own character and are a testimony to Himself.

Thus, beginning even in the Old Testament, the tenor and fabric of the biblical faith is a faith that honors the patriarchs. Israel is identified as the people of Abraham and Isaac and Jacob. The nation is like unto a family, as we see in the language of Numbers 12:7 (NASB), "My household," and "My family." God is as the Father to the nation.

The Lord speaks of Israel as "my firstborn" in Exodus 4:22. This is a central biblical motif. And we are told to honor father and mother. Consider this one hermeneutical question: How does the relationship of a child to a parent weave throughout the fabric of Scripture from Genesis to Revelation? You will find this relationship pictured throughout the Bible. You find it in the didactic material, with very clear rules, regulations, and precepts that reveal how children and parents are to be properly related. It is also in the historical narratives of Scripture, where to dishonor a parent is to bring dishonor upon the entire nation. And, of course, it is found in the wisdom literature, with endless exhortations from Solomon to his son to walk in obedience. "Honor your father and your mother, that your days may be long in the land that the Lord your God is giving you" (Exodus 20:12).

MODERN ATTITUDES

Now, this is a very different concept from our own times. Just consider what happened in France in 2004. As a heat wave spread throughout Europe, fifteen thousand elderly persons died in France alone. What shamed the nation is that many thousands of those elderly parents who were allowed to die were abandoned in their homes. Their bodies were left in their homes as their children and grandchildren went on family vacation without interruption, neglecting to take care of their own grandparents and parents.

The French have now made this a matter of national law. Article 207 of the French civil code now says that adult children are legally responsible for their elderly parents. Why does it take a civil act of the French government to tell children that they are to honor mother and father? Infractions of the law are to be met with fines and possible imprisonment. But laws cannot fix this problem. The problem is something deeply imbedded in the human heart. To abandon father and mother is to dishonor the Creator who made us.

Another problem is the lack of a biblical, long-term vision for the family. The biblical vision is of father and mother and children. The biblical vision is of the father taking the lead for a transgenerational vision for his family. Even in many Christian homes today, parents often see their responsibility in terms of getting children from infancy to graduation from college. Then they think their job is done. That is the horizon of our responsibility.

The biblical vision, however, is of the father taking responsibility, not merely for his children, but for his grandchildren and countless generations to come. The absence of this vision explains why much of the family ministry in our churches is so superficial, so ineffective, and so wrongly directed. At best, it is focused on short-term problem solving, not transgenerational problem solving.

ROLE, RESPONSE, AND REALITY

So what is the proper role of parents, the proper response of children, and the proper reality of the church when it comes to honoring our parents? First, the proper role of parents is not mere biology. Parenting, biblically defined and summarized, includes the responsibility to love, to care for, to provide, to nurture, to protect, to teach, and to discipline. It is not just to raise useful citizens for the society. It is not just to get the next generation to a point of maturity so that they can continue the biological progression of the race. It is to raise children in the nurture and admonition of the Lord so that they would bring glory to father and mother, because in doing so they will bring glory to the Creator God.

Ursinus, commenting on the Heidelberg Catechism's teaching on the Ten Commandments, uses two beautiful expressions—*schoolmaster* and *magistrate*—to speak of the Scriptural responsibility of parents to their children.

THE PARENT AS SCHOOLMASTER

First, to be a Christian parent is to teach. Recalling Deuteronomy 6, we are to teach our children "when [we] sit in [our] house, and when [we] walk by the way, and when [we] lie down, and when [we] rise" (verse 7). We must seize every opportunity to teach. This includes formal didactic teaching and the modeling that takes place between parent and child. This parental responsibility to teach should be intentional, didactic, constant, consistent, and it is to be repeated. In Israel, teaching functioned like this: The child raised in the covenant home was to be told from the very beginning: "You are a part of this promise because you are a part of this family. As part of this promise, you are to learn to live as a child of this promise so that your days may be prolonged in the land the Lord your God has given you."

Memory also plays a vital part in teaching. Thinking back to Joshua 4, when a covenant child asked a parent to explain the rules, statutes, and commandments, the parent was to explain how they had been slaves to the Pharaoh in Egypt. When a son comes and asks, "What do these stones mean?"—the memorial stones of Joshua 4—he would be told the story of how God brought out His people from a land of bondage to a land of promise. A parent would say something like this:

"We were slaves to Pharaoh in Egypt, but God brought us out in order that He might bring us in, in order that He might show His name to be great. He put us in this land for His glory, and we are to live as His people, and thus it is a natural thing that we are to learn His laws and His statutes and His commandments. How else will we know them? How else will we live them? How else will we realize the purpose for which we were brought into this land of promise? How else will we be prolonged here? As the book of Deuteronomy makes clear, if we disobey, we will be taken off of this land, and we will be led into captivity by other nations. And captivity will be our national humiliation and our disgrace. You are a child of promise."

In Judaism, teaching was primarily the function of the father. Thus, you have masculine terms repeated in the text. The father was to teach. The father was to ensure both the transmission of tradition (the pattern of habits we follow) and truth (the pattern of reality we have come to know, by God's grace).

A Christian home is to be the first school, the first church, and the first government.

Mothers, too, are involved here. It is interesting as you read the Old Testament that you come across these wonderful passages of patriarchal significance. You think of the relationship between Joseph and Jacob, even to the stewardship of a father's bones. It continued also in the New Testament, accompanied by sweet passages of a mother's love. Paul writing to Timothy in 2 Timothy 3:15 reminds him that he has known these things from childhood, he has been taught them rightly. In 2 Timothy 1:5, he says, "I am reminded of your sincere faith, a faith that dwelt first in your grandmother Lois and your mother Eunice and now, I am sure, dwells in you as well." Fathers are key. Mothers are crucial in the transfer of doctrine, in the inculcation of a worldview, in the remembrance of a story, and in the dependence upon Scripture.

A Christian home is to be the first school, the first church, and the first government. The father and the mother are to be as schoolmasters in the home. It is our responsibility to make sure that our children are knowledgeable about the Word of God. It is to the shame of any Christian father or mother that the children of the home would be ignorant and immature in knowing the things of God. How many of our churches truly preach and teach the responsibilities of parents to teach the Scripture, to make certain that their children are knowledgeable in Scripture?

Instead, in contemporary youth ministry, we hire someone to entertain. In so many churches, we simply don't expect parents to teach their children, so we will attempt to do it for them. We say, "Just franchise it out. Send your kids to us, and we will teach them what you will not and perhaps even cannot teach because you have not been taught yourselves." This is the administration of self-made orphans.

Instead, the church should direct itself to the kind of youth ministry that not only reaches youth but also teaches parents how to fulfill the responsibility of a father and mother as the schoolmasters of the home. The transfer of doctrine, the structure and fabric of truth—this must be taught, for it will not be received by the child through osmosis. Intentional instruction and precept must lead the way, followed by a modeling out of behavior and practice.

> The transfer of doctrine will not be received by the child through osmosis.

We must also inculcate a Christian worldview in our children, even as they are learning the overall story of the history of redemption and come to a saving knowledge of Jesus Christ as Savior and Lord. Just as no child in Israel was to be ignorant of the story of the Exodus and God's covenant with His people, so also our children must be deeply immersed in the Christian narrative. We want them to know the Bible's story of how "God so loved the world, that he gave his only Son, that whoever believes in Him should not perish but have eternal life" (John 3:16). They must know the story of God's creation of a people through the blood of His Son, for the glory of His own name—a people who can defy death and will live forever with Him. This is to be their inheritance from the Word of God.

THE PARENT AS MAGISTRATE

But father and mother are not only schoolmasters; they are magistrates, the dispensers of discipline to their children. Discipline is not very popular in contemporary parenting. However, those of us raised in Christian homes know that our parents could together be described as judge, jury, and executioner. It is an inescapable parental responsibility to discipline the child, a fact revealed in Scripture. A rebellious, disobedient, disorderly, untaught, unruly child is a terrible curse upon a family.

Again, to our shame, this is not taught as much as it should be in our churches. The influence of our therapeutic age teaches parents to be extremely careful not to impose their will upon the child. Our psychologized society believes children basically would be healthy but for parents. The scriptural worldview is very different—our little darling is born in sin. He may look innocent, and she is no doubt cute, but that child is a sinner whose heart is planning treason.

Our psychologized age also says that parents should not seek external conformity in our children, preferring internal self-actualization as the goal. Thinking back on my own childhood, my parents were not greatly concerned with my "internal self-actualization." The Christian parent understands that external conformity is the very least that is to be expected. Informed by Scripture, Christian parents understand that the internal alignment of the soul is instructed by the external conformity of the body. The parent knows the struggle. You wish you could get into the heart. You wish you could reach down into the deep, inner caverns of the soul. And yet, perhaps the most you can do is to force bodily obedience. That is at least a start.

The Scripture teaches that the father who loves his son disciplines his son. In Proverbs 23:10, Israel is warned not to go into "the fields of the fatherless." And immediately thereafter, we read, "Do not withhold discipline from a child; if you strike him with a rod, he will not die. If you strike him with the rod, you will save his soul from Sheol" (verses 13–14).

In this generation of undisciplined children, many people consider corporal punishment to be some kind of throwback to an oppressive age. In Scripture, corporal punishment is the responsibility of the Christian parent, to teach with the rod. As a biblical principle, the physical pain of justice meted out by the parental magistrate standing in the place of God is a teacher that reaches the soul. Children must learn cause and effect. They must be taught even bodily the difference between obedience and disobedience. The pain of corporal punishment makes progressively clear to young children that there is a law, a judge, and there is justice. Cause and effect. Disobedience and obedience.

Premeditated treason against parental authority must be shut down or the insurrection will spread!

A recent article in *USA Today* profiled successful CEOs of large companies, and discovered that most of them were spanked as children. It is a stunning realization to many readers of *USA Today* that those who have worked their way into positions of leadership were spanked as children. There must be a psychological lesson there, and indeed there is. But there is also a theological lesson, because the seat of learning is a means of reaching the heart and the soul, and parents understand this.

In Australia, although the government developed programs to discourage parents from spanking their children, parents still spank. They conducted a poll among Australian mothers and found that 80 percent of them believe in spanking—the number goes up to 90 percent for mothers of young children. I have met these who said, "I would never spank my children," but it was a hypothetical declaration because they had no children. The view usually changes when the married couple actually have children. The spirit of defiance shows up in the face of the child. The parent knows that this sorry attitude is not just an accident. This is premeditated treason against parental authority, and it will either be shut down or the insurrection will spread!

The father and mother are magistrates, an image of the relationship between God and His own people. In Hebrews 12, a father's discipline is described in just this way. After we read about faith and are told to look to the example of Jesus, we then read about the discipline of a father's love. We are told that we are to expect this. Indeed, we are to seek this. Parents who love are parents who discipline. Hear the author of Hebrews:

> It is for discipline that you have to endure. God is treating you as sons. For what son is there whom his father does not discipline? If you are left without discipline, in which all have participated, then you are illegitimate children and not sons. Besides this, we have had earthly fathers who disciplined us and we respected them. Shall we not much more be subject to the Father of spirits and live? For they disciplined us for a short time as it seemed best to them, but he disciplines us for our good, that we may share his holiness. For the moment all discipline seems painful rather than pleasant, but later it yields the peaceful fruit of righteousness to those who have been trained by it. (Hebrews 12:7–11)

We are told that discipline "yields the peaceful fruit of righteousness." The parent stands in a position of authority that ultimately points to God. As Calvin wrote, "God calls us to Himself through our parents. We learn to be subject to God by learning to be subject to our parents, and parental discipline teaches us how to be disciplined by the Father."[2] And Hodge once explained, "Parents stand in relationship to their dependent children as, so to speak, in the place of God."[3]

We are to receive this. The Christian father is the patriarch and the Christian mother is the matriarch of the society, passing down the Christian faith and tradition by fulfilling their responsibility to be schoolmaster and magistrate.

THE PROPER RESPONSE OF CHILDREN

The proper response of children is very clear in this text. Children are to honor. This means to respect, to love, to obey, and to respond with obligation to parents. This is a fundamental duty. Not merely giving external obedience, children are to know and to desire the approval and glory of the father and mother on earth. The word *honor* is much more comprehensive than the word *obey*. Obedience is the starting point, but children honor father and mother by the internal inclination of the heart to desire what the father and mother desire. This is how children are to receive the patrimony, by honoring father and mother with every dimension of life. This is a basic pattern for life for those in submission to Scripture.

In Scripture, one of the greatest curses is a disobedient or a rebellious son. Augustine asked, "If anyone fails to honor his parents, is there anyone he will spare?"[4] Those who would dishonor parents would dishonor the government, would dishonor authority, and would dishonor God. When Jesus gave us a parabolic picture of the gospel, He illustrated the desperate wickedness of human sin by portraying a son, a "prodigal son," who forsakes his living father and goes into a far country to spend his prematurely gained inheritance. In stark contrast, however, the proper response of children is to obey.

The Puritans rightly taught that a child should be the parent's echo. When the father speaks, the child should echo back obedience. If something else is echoed back, it is something displeasing to God.

And as in Israel, so also in the church; in Ephesians 6, we read that children are to obey their parents. As the apostle Paul cites the Fifth Commandment, notice that he universalizes it: "Children, obey your parents in the Lord, for this is right. Honor your father and mother (which is the first commandment with a promise), so that it may be well with you, and that you may live long on the earth" (verses 1–3 NASB). This is not just a command for the people of the promise living in the Land of Promise, but is for everywhere God's people are found—parents are to be obeyed.

> *In* caring for our parents we teach our own children what covenantal faithfulness looks like.

Beyond God's covenant people who would enter the covenant land of Canaan, this commandment is also addressed to God's new covenant people, the church. The promise still pertains.

We are to honor the father and the mother by honoring their name. We are to bring honor to the patrimony that we have received by our behavior, by our deportment, by our covenantal faithfulness, by our embrace of all that has been given us in this patrimony. And in testimony to the fact that we consider it our greatest honor to be our father and mother's child, we continue to pass down the inheritance that we have received from them.

Such testimony to our parents includes giving them care. In the new demographic reality of the sandwich generation, we are reminded that most of us who were cared for by our parents will care for our parents, and God's glory is in it. God's glory is in it because in caring for our parents we show the world and we teach our own children what covenantal faithfulness looks like in the obligation of children to parents. It is not just care and provision; it is honor.

In honoring our parents, we bring honor to God. The world does not think this way. Philosopher Jane English once asked this question:

what do grown children owe their parents? She said, "I will contend that the answer is nothing." Speaking of the contemporary picture, she said, "We have learned mutuality, we have learned that the responsibility is that parents should earn the friendship of their children and parents who do not earn the friendship of their children deserve no mutuality."[5] Such thinking is antithetical to the biblical worldview, which teaches that we never outgrow our parents.

Sigmund Freud said it is our psychological responsibility to kill off the father—liberating ourselves from bondage to parental expectations. And Freud lives on in the spirit of our age. Although entertainment and literature would have us "kill off the father," the biblical worldview teaches that we honor the father. Nothing could be more counterrevolutionary than that. This comes with a promise that obedience and honor to our parents will lead to living long in the land. And, as Paul would have us realize, he is not just speaking about our earthly lives, he is talking about the promise that comes to us by God's gift of eternal life.

THE PROPER REALITY OF THE CHURCH

Third, we must acknowledge that there are some who have not orphaned themselves, but who nonetheless are orphaned. Sometimes unfaithful parents have made their children spiritual orphans with no one in their life that is unto them as father and mother. Do you realize then, just how rich the picture is in the New Testament of the church as the people of God? God's new covenant people are, as it were, a new family. The church is the household of faith, made up of a people adopted by God into His family.

The text of Numbers 12:6–7 is echoed in Hebrews 3:1–6, as we are told that the church is now God's household. The church is the household of God through Christ—this is the new family. Thus, in the church, we have not only the responsibility to honor our fathers and our mothers, but there is in the church no one who is to be an orphan. As a new covenant people, everyone in the church has a father and everyone has a mother, because we are as brothers and sisters to each other—a family to each other. Paul instructs Timothy and Titus that young men are to honor the older men, and older women are to counsel younger women. In the church, no one is to be left an orphan. The church itself is a family being built up into a household of faith, honoring not only biological parents but also patriarchs and matriarchs, living and dead.

God's new covenant people must receive this as a gift. Just as there are no orphans in the church, there must not be any abandoned and dishonored mother or father. Within the church, we care for those who are the aged among us because they are the honored among us. The church that fails to demonstrate this by the richness of its life as the new family of faith is a church that dishonors the gospel of God.

The great Puritan pastor Thomas Watson said that honoring our spiritual fathers means that we must give them respect, we must become advocates for them, and we must be conformed to their doctrine. Is this not rich? Think of the heritage we have from the halls of church history. We respect the patriarchs and matriarchs who are God's gifts to us. We become advocates for them. We save them from the dishonor of an age that dishonors all things old. We become advocates for them by remembering their names with honor, and by making sure that even though their memory may be erased from the rest of the earth, their memory is not erased here.

We look back to Abraham and Isaac and Jacob, to Paul and Peter and Stephen, to Ruth and Lois and Eunice. We look back to Athanasius and Augustine, to Zwingli, Knox, Luther, Calvin. We look back to Edwards and Wesley and Whitefield. We look back to Carey and Spurgeon and Moody. We look back because we dare not look forward without first looking back.

"Honor your father and your mother, that your days may be long in the land that the Lord your God is giving you." We desperately need to hear this, and God's glory is in it.

The SIXTH COMMANDMENT

You shall not murder.

~ Exodus 20:13

6

The Sanctity of Life and the Violence of Sin

The Sixth Commandment is blessedly simple: "You shall not murder," or as many of us memorized this commandment in the King James Version: "Thou shalt not kill." Looking at the Ten Commandments, these Ten Words, we are reminded that these are words addressed to Israel, God's chosen people, the covenant nation. Yet these are words that even now instruct and guide us as members of Christ's sanctified church.

The Holy Spirit uses these Ten Words to shape our hearts. Even as those who no longer live under the law, the law addressed to Israel in the covenant of old, we do live under the law of Christ. And Christ's law is a liberating law, a law that will take us even deeper into the heart of murder than the act of murder itself.

As the Ten Commandments are explained, injury is often done to the final five commandments by suggesting that the simplicity of interpretation comes down to the fact that they pertain to our relationships with fellow human beings. Although that statement is true, the fuller truth is that our responsibility to our fellow human beings is grounded entirely in our relationship with God. Because of our fidelity to God's law, our submission to God's sovereignty, and our knowledge of God's purposes, we see human beings in an entirely different light. And herein is the radical truth—without the first five commandments, everything we learn in the second table of the law is continuously and ruinously negotiable. If you take away the first five commandments, then everything that follows can be redefined and renegotiated. The frame of reference, no longer transcendent, becomes merely temporal. Human life has no claim to human dignity other than what we humans choose to ascribe to it.

But we do not read the Sixth Commandment and those that follow without having been taught and instructed by the first five. Our responsibility to God, our Creator, summons us to these next five commandments. In them we see a picture and reminder and a clear teaching of how we must relate to each other if we are to glorify God, honoring Him and giving Him His due.

"You shall not murder." In the original context, those who were joined together in covenant with God's people must not murder a fellow Israelite. And yet because of the *imago Dei*, the image of God, in which mankind is made, this commandment is universalized to all human beings. Human beings have no right to murder.

This text is often described in terms of reverence for life, a term popularized by theological scholar Albert Schweitzer in his book of the same name. Schweitzer's idea of reverence for life was very popular,

> The worth of human life is grounded in the Creator rather than in the creature.

coming as it did during the twentieth century when so little of this reverence was found. But we should note that this commandment is not about a generalized or a generic reverence for life. Instead this reverence is for life made in the image of God, with the dignity and the worth of that life grounded in the Creator rather than in the creature. When we try to speak of a reverence for life in terms of a humanistic, secular naturalistic understanding, we quickly end up talking about a reverence for *certain* kinds of life, for *certain* kinds of human beings. And we follow a logic that leads to death.

THE UNAUTHORIZED, MALICIOUS TAKING OF LIFE

This is explicitly about our duty to God. This very short commandment gets speedily to the point: "You shall not murder." The Hebrew word for *murder* is used thirteen times in the Bible, and here it clearly refers to the fact that we are forbidden to murder each other, to kill unauthorized or with malice. But this verb also can be extended to manslaughter, or unintentional homicide that is negligent in its form. We shall see that the Scripture speaks to both of these in terms of our responsibility and culpability.

Preachers have difficulty with this particular commandment because the other nine commands seem to be so universally applicable to human temptations and to human realities. But when we look at "Thou shall not murder," it is easy to think ourselves distant from this particular commandment. It is very easy to abstract this commandment so it no longer has the bite, the kind of command and sense of authority and immediate address as the other nine do. How many murderers are there in our midst? And yet, there is no question that this commandment is addressed to us.

Indeed it is dangerous and false to put distance and abstraction between ourselves and this commandment. The unauthorized, malicious, and intentional killing of human beings takes place all around us. Homicide rates are indicative of this. Another indicator, though not reported in the crime statistics, is carnage that takes place through abortion, the wanton malicious taking of life.

In the twentieth century, we found out that murder could be accomplished on a massive scale. Writing in his book *Out of Control*, Zbigniew Brzezinski, national security director for President Jimmy Carter, said that the twentieth century could best be characterized by the word "mega-death." He chronicled the actual scale of carnage in the twentieth century, and using very objective numbers, Brzezinski suggests that four human beings alone could be blamed for 175 million deaths: Hitler, Lenin, Stalin, and Mao. During the final century of the second millennium AD, murder, mayhem, and carnage all expanded on such a large scale that it defies imagination. The figure of 175 million deaths traceable to just those four dictators exceeds the populations of the United Kingdom and France combined; it approaches two-thirds of the population of the United States at the end of the twentieth century.

What do we say to this? The twentieth century leaves memories of murder that can never be forgotten. Even now there are those, still living, who were the youngest survivors of the Nazi death camps. Fewer in number each year, they live with tattooed numbers, etched on their forearm as well as their minds, numbers that marked them for death.

We are the surviving successors of a century that learned how to kill on a massive scale: the gulags, the Holocaust, the killing fields of Cambodia, the slaughter of Rwanda and the Sudan, an entire industry of death. New words like *genocide* were created to describe a level of carnage that did not exist prior to the twentieth century.

VIOLENT DEATH IN THE
TWENTIETH AND TWENTY-FIRST CENTURIES

In his book *The Age of Extremes*, historian Eric Hobsbawm speaks of what he calls "the short twentieth century," a massive social transformation in the entire world picture between World War I and the fall of the Berlin Wall. The one thing most notable about this, as he writes with a great deal of pessimism, is that it was an age of sheer catastrophe and ritualized industrial-scale death.[1]

At the end of World War I, Winston Churchill remarked that those who were involved in the leadership of that war, on both sides, came to such a point of desperation that they would nearly stop short of nothing. They gassed each other, they killed each other in a massive scale by the millions, and most of those who died were young men between the ages of eighteen and thirty. Churchill said they only held themselves back from ritualistic torture and he wondered, had the war not ended, how long that prohibition would have held.[2] We consider ourselves sophisticated people, as did Europeans in the early twentieth century, thinking themselves the most civilized people who had ever yet existed. Yet what they did was to perfect killing. It tells us a great deal about what it means to live in a world this side of Genesis 3. There is no distance.

Even in the first decade of the twenty-first century, there is murder on the streets. Violent death is a leading story on our news. It is a leading cause of death for young males, especially for those in this society in certain ethnic groups and cultural contexts. And yet it is not just that. There is also murder on the small and large screen. By the age of eighteen the average American child has seen more than eighty thousand murders depicted on television, film, and in video games. The video games add up the carnage faster than any form of electronic medium. Lieutenant Colonel David Grossman, who taught marksmanship for the United States Army, was called upon to suggest why young boys who had never fired a real gun before could walk into a high school and kill with military precision. And he pointed out that video games were turning young American males into trained killers, with an instinct for a trigger and with an eye for an aim unlike anything any military force had ever seen before. Having never shot a gun in malice, they can murder with military precision.

We are making murder so routine that it is now something that is expected and is no longer taken with great moral seriousness. It is merely the pretext for the drama yet to unfold on the screen or the story to be replayed thousands and thousands of times over with a controller in hand. There is no distance.

But the most important reason why we must recognize that there is no distance with the Sixth Commandment is what we really do not want to admit to each other. And that is that we are not distant from this command because we really are capable of this act. It is very easy for us to say we would never resort to violence, certainly not to lethal force! And for most of us, that is probably true, but would it be true under circumstances we cannot yet now envision? Would it be true if we really knew our own hearts as our Creator knows our hearts? There is no distance.

There is also no abstraction. Many preachers try to make this commandment into something like the Golden Rule: "Murder not, that thou not be murdered." Some even make this into a generalized prescription for benevolence towards our fellow human beings, a commandment for a generalized spirit of good feelings. But that is not what the commandment is about! When the Lord wrote these words on tablets of stone, He wrote "murder!" It is murder that is the issue.

A CONTROVERSY: GOD AUTHORIZED KILLING

Now here we encounter a controversy. How do we translate and interpret this commandment? It seems simple enough, yet we have two different major translations and traditions and the English translation heritage. There is the King James Version, "Thou shalt not kill," and then of more modern translations, "You shall not murder." The Hebrew word used here means *murder, manslaughter, violent and unauthorized killing*. We need to approach this with theological candor and with Christian honesty, and admit to each other that there is a great deal of killing in the Bible. We also need to admit with equal candor that God is doing a great deal of the killing in the Bible. This is a blood-drenched book. The Bible, in its honesty, speaks of these things with directness; there is killing by war and killing by execution.

Among the many descriptions of God in the Old Testament, we find that He is a God of war, and thus in the Old Testament there is authorized killing, even commanded killing, especially as found in the two categories of war and capital punishment. Here you face a question of your own theological integrity and your own spiritual courage.

You either believe this or not. You either believe in the inspiration and inerrancy of the Old Testament text, or you believe that this is merely a corruption of some ancient people's understanding of a violent and cruel God. Those are your options.

God has avenged His own name and His own glory with the taking of blood.

Several years ago while delivering a series of lectures at a theological seminary, a prominent pastor stood up before the students and declared that the God who commanded the destruction of the Amalekites is not the same God who was the Father of the Lord Jesus Christ. Well if that pastor is correct, then we are in big trouble. Let us understand that this is the Word of God, and it is for our good and for our instruction. The God who saves sinners through the blood of the Lord Jesus Christ is a God who has avenged His own name and His own glory with the taking of blood.

Those who suggest that it should be translated "Thou shalt not kill" are looking for a universal command that would prohibit capital punishment, and a reinterpretation of our understanding of the rules of war. What are those rules of war? What do we say when we follow the one described as the Prince of Peace? Well, for one thing, we had better read the New Testament as well as the Old, because if your problem is killing, to be very honest, there is more eschatological death yet to come that is revealed in the New Testament than anything accumulated in the Old Testament and in all the centuries of human experience since then. God is not a pacifist.

Now lest we assume from that that we have the same warrant to kill as does He, let us be reminded that God is in heaven and we are not. Therefore, let our words be few, and let our obedience to His command be humble.

What do we say about war? When we read the Bible clearly, war was a part of God's plan for the conquest of the Holy Land, the Land of Promise. And war throughout human experience has been a perpetual necessity and a ruinous tragedy. Historians have been engaged in various seminars and debates and arguments over whether or not at any time in the history of humanity there has been a state of peace. With a Eurocentric view, historians in the nineteenth century tried to point back to a relatively few number of years when Europe was at peace, but again that peace did not mean there was no killing whatsoever, even state-sponsored killing. It meant only that there was no nation-state that was currently in a declared state of war with one of its neighbors.

A JUST WAR?

The Christian church has had to try to deal with this, and this led to the development of what is known as just-war theory. If war is going to happen, and if sometimes war is *the least worst option*, we must understand as Christians that there has to be some kind of rubric for moral reasoning that would enable us to know that this is an authorized war. Thus, just-war theory covers such issues as how a war would be declared just before it is fought, and then how war would be justly prosecuted after it has been rightly declared. Just-war theory requires that a legitimate authority declare the war. It requires that the war be defensive rather than offensive.

The theory comes down to this: All previous things having been tried, war becomes the only option that will actually save more lives than it takes. If you start looking at the moral calculus, even before the war has begun, then you realize how difficult this question is. And then you look at just-war theory in terms of the actual conduct and prosecution of the war, and you understand the responsibility to have legitimate authority that discriminates between combatants and noncombatants.

But the twentieth century taught us that war is not so easily controlled and limited. The realities of modern warfare make applying just-war principles very difficult. Looking back, we can see that even

World War II—a war made necessary in order to defend life and liberty—was a war also filled with horror and matters of moral confusion. This is even more the case with reference to more recent wars—much less than wars of the future.

What about a war as clearly justified as World War II? We know now about the death camps of Treblinka and Birkenau. We know now about things that the Americans did not know when the war started, and there is controversy about how much was known even when the war ended. But we do know this: during that war we too decided to blur the distinction between combatants and noncombatants. Ask the citizens of Hamburg, rained upon by millions of tons of bombs from the Eighth Air Force. Ask the citizens of Dresden, one of the most cultured cities in Europe, which was crushed under the incendiary weight of millions of tons of bombs. In the twentieth century, the idea of strategic bombing began to make sense. The goal was to break the enemy's industrial capacity, and thus his ability and will to fight, but that meant not only destroying factories but the cities around those factories and the people who worked within those factories, the aged and the infants along with the workers and their wives.

I am thankful that Hitler's Third Reich was ground into the dust. I am thankful that Allied Forces defeated the forces of the Axis powers, and especially the Third Reich. But we cannot look back even to that war, as necessary as it was, the least worst option under the circumstances, and think that we emerged from that war with our hands clean.

So, too, with the War on Terror early in this century—a series of skirmishes that former Secretary of Defense Donald Rumsfeld has called "asymmetrical warfare." How does just-war theory rightly apply to this? How does just-war theory, in terms of how war would be developed and lethal force would be authorized and prosecuted—how does that work when any given teenager with a backpack could be a suicide bomber?

The commandment states, "You shall not murder." We need to recognize just how difficult it is to have our hands clean of murder, even though we think ourselves immune and clear.

A SANCTIONING OF CAPITAL PUNISHMENT?

Capital punishment is also authorized in the Bible, seen explicitly in the Old Testament where there are over a dozen offenses that the Lord declares to be worthy of death. Capital punishment is ordered under those circumstances in order to make the severity of the crime clear and understood. There is significant protection built in for the people of Israel, lest a false accusation would lead to a false execution and a wrongful death. As a matter of fact, the protections provided for those in Israel who are charged with murder or capital offense exceeded those provided in Western legal tradition.

But capital punishment is not an abstract issue in the Bible. In Romans 13:4 we are told that the governing authority "does not bear the sword in vain." There is no way around what that text is telling us; capital punishment is part of God's plan. The Noahic covenant of Genesis 9:6 reads, "Whoever sheds the blood of man, by man shall his blood be shed, for God made man in his own image." Murder is an insult to God. Murder deprives God of one who was made in His image and for His glory. Murder is the arrogant, willful subtraction of God's glory, and the capacity for the display of God's glory in the midst of His creation. Although that would be true of ravaging a forest, burning a garden, or desecrating nature, far more when the one who is killed bears the image of God. It is a personal attack upon the dignity of the Creator.

> We speak of murder as harm to the victim. But the main harm is to the dignity of God Himself.

The killer or the murderer becomes the taker of the gift of life, the image destroyer. In the Western legal tradition, we speak of murder as harm to the victim, the victim's friends and family and circle of acquaintances. But in the Scripture, the main harm is not to the victim nor to the victim's friends and family, but rather to the dignity of God Himself.

There are some who want to argue that we must now reinterpret this commandment to be a generalized statement about reverence for life, that all killing is wrong, including all war and capital punishment—even killing in self-defense. So argues Wilma Ann Bailey in her book *"You Shall Not Kill" or "You Shall Not Murder"?* When I first saw this book. I wanted to know how the author could come to argue for "you shall not kill" rather than "you shall not murder," and especially how she would handle the canonical witness of Scripture. In the Old Testament itself there are very clear references to war and capital punishment, not only allowed but commanded by God.

The only way you can make this argument that all killing is wrong is to select certain verses from the Bible and reject others. This so-called "canon within the canon" implies that certain texts in the Bible are more inspired than others. That's Bailey's approach. Consider this passage from the book:

> Some who reject a kill translation for Exodus 20:13 think that "the Bible" as it exists today was one entity in ancient times. The Bible in the opinion of most modern critical scholars is not a single unified entity, but a collection of diverse materials with diverse theological viewpoints. The ancient Israelites struggled with questions of how to understand God and God's relationship with humankind. Modern scholars generally reject attempts at harmonizing texts in favor of placing them in their own contexts whether literary or historical, sociological or theological. Yes, a killing theology emerges in some texts, but those texts need not theologically trump non-killing texts. Even where a penalty of death is stated in the Bible, often the question arises of who if anyone is to carry out the penalty. . . . Many modern commentators place that authority in the hands of the state or the nation even though such entities did not exist in ancient times and would not have been in the mind of the biblical author. Moreover, biblically speaking, if God reserves the right to kill, this did not mean that humans have the same right. The infamous phrase

from Genesis 9:6, "The one who sheds the blood of a human by human, his blood will be shed," is nearly always read as a command for capital punishment. More likely, this is a reflection on the escalation of violence—the way of bloodshed only leads to more bloodshed. This statement need not be read as a command. No imperative is used.

"Scripture interprets Scripture" proponents also point to the books of Joshua and Judges as proof that killing is permitted in the Hebrew Bible. This is particularly disturbing. Few scholars, rabbis, or pastors point to those books as models of appropriate behavior. Indeed, the critique that appears at the end of Judges, "In those days there was no king in Israel, everyone did what was right in his or her eyes," appears to be an ancient criticism of the violence and mayhem described earlier in that book, and perhaps in the book of Joshua as well.

Further, people tend to assume that according to the Bible, God commanded a battle or a killing when in fact the text never indicates that God had anything to do with killing. Moreover, within the Bible, there are summary statements of ethical principles that in the mind of some biblical traditions are superior to other guidelines.[3]

What Professor Bailey has done here is to misuse Exodus 20:13 and to invalidate other texts from the Bible. She argues that some biblical teachings are "superior to other guidelines." Where does this end?

We must understand that "You shall not kill" is not a blanket prohibition against killing. Instead, it is a prohibition against unauthorized killing through murder or manslaughter. Whether by premeditated intent or by negligence, the taking of life is a matter of deadly significance. In Israel, if you are building a house, there is a warning to not fail to put a parapet around the roof as a safety precaution against someone falling off (Deuteronomy 22:8). If a death occurred because of your neglect in this duty, you bring bloodshed upon your house. Although there is no malice toward any particular individual, and thus no first-degree homicide, there is negligence and antipathy toward the entire human race by that negligence. According to the logic of Scripture, those who would fail to save a life are guilty of a crime against life.

Now the commandment begins to come into focus. We begin to understand how the Sixth Commandment functioned in ancient Israel. We begin to understand that it was a rule against the taking of human life when the taking of that life was not explicitly authorized by God. As one recent commentator has said, one of the scariest things we hear these days from some people in the church is that it is dangerous to kill in the name of God.[4] This commentator concludes that we should be far more afraid of any killing that is *not* in the name of God, because only that killing which He would allow or command is legitimate. Everything else is an affront to His dignity and a denial of His glory through the destruction of His image by the wanton, willful, intentional attempt to destroy that image in another human being.

> "**You** shall not kill" is a prohibition against unauthorized killing through murder or manslaughter.

JESUS ON THE SIXTH COMMANDMENT

And yet, as important as the historical and textual analysis is, we read these words as Christians, and so we cannot read Exodus without reading Matthew. We cannot read the Ten Commandments without reading the Sermon on the Mount. And there we are reminded of the formula so often found in Matthew 5, where Jesus says: "You have heard that the ancients were told . . ." or "You have heard that is was said . . .", followed by "But I say to you . . ." (verses 21 and 22; 27 and 28; 33 and 34; 38 and 39; 43 and 44 NASB). As Jesus introduces this major section on the Sermon on the Mount, He says:

Do not think that I came to abolish the Law or the Prophets; I did not come to abolish but to fulfill. For truly I say to you, until heaven and earth pass away, not the smallest letter or stroke shall pass from the Law until all is accomplished. Whoever then annuls one of the least of these commandments, and teaches others to do the same, shall be called least in the kingdom of heaven; but whoever keeps and teaches them, he shall be called great in the kingdom of heaven. (verses 17–19 NASB)

Not to annul, but to fulfill? What does that look like? Speaking of the command against murder, Jesus said,

You have heard that the ancients were told, "You shall not commit murder" and "Whoever commits murder shall be liable to the court." But I say to you that everyone who is angry with his brother shall be guilty before the court; and whoever says to his brother, "You good-for-nothing," shall be guilty before the supreme court; and whoever says, "You fool," shall be guilty enough to go into the fiery hell. (verses 21–22 NASB)

We previously said that there really is no distance between ourselves and this commandment, and now Jesus' words help us understand the immediacy of these words. The Sixth Commandment seemed comfortably distant from us, if all that was really at stake was the actual, premeditated murder of another human being! Very few of us, by the restraining power of God's law and grace, are going to become a premeditated murderer. The reality is that murder is not something most of us find as a personal struggle. Then we read Matthew 5 and see that murder is no longer a matter merely of the external taking of life by knife or club or stone or gun—it is also anger and hatred.

If we read carefully the Old Testament, even there we find murder being described in terms of a root of hatred and anger. Now Jesus takes this even deeper. Now, as we are under the law of Christ, we come to understand that it is not as though we are suddenly freed from the law. We bear the awful knowledge that our heart is a murderous heart! We know that hatred and anger lurk all too close to us in our own human heart. Admitting that is a good thing.

In the Old Testament, to avoid violating the Sixth Commandment and to show a basic respect for life, you only had to refrain from murder or negligent homicide. As such, it is not difficult to conceive of our perfect obedience to the command. But when we read Matthew 5, we are in big trouble. We understand that human anger is a complex force, burning hot in some and cold in others. In some people, anger is ready to strike out all the time, but in others it sits dormant. Because we are on this side of Genesis 3, it is always there. The commandment of Christ interiorizes the sin and radicalizes the command—not only are we under responsibility to Genesis 9:6 and Exodus 20:13, but also to Matthew 5:21–22.

> Our heart is a murderous heart! Hatred and anger lurk all too close to us.

Now we must refuse to carry around the malice and hatred that would deny the dignity of those at whom we would hurl venomous words. Jesus Himself, later in the Gospels, refers to persons as "fools," so the heart is the issue here, rather than the specific word. It is an evil heart that would jump all too quickly from irritation to anger to hatred to murder.

We also need to understand and admit our corporate responsibility. Israel is at times described as bearing corporately a bloodguilt. And if that be so of Israel, it must be so also of those of us who would ignore the carnage around us, the carnage for example, of abortion. Over forty-five million unborn Americans have been killed in the womb since the Supreme Court sanctioned the practice in 1973 (Roe v. Wade). Abortion is now a routine medical procedure under the moral logic of personal autonomy and a woman's right to choose. The

American College of Obstetricians and Gynecologists has suggested that all pregnant women need to be tested for Down syndrome and other indicators in the fetus—the obvious implication being that the right thing then to do would be to destroy the fetus in the womb.

THE AGE OF MEGADEATH AND MICRODEATH

We are also facing a whole new reality as we live surrounded by clinics with frozen human embryos, millions to be destroyed either by active malice or by passive allowance. Once again, we face a very difficult question here. If that embryo is not a human being, if it does not possess full human dignity, then where along the continuum of that embryo until the end of life and elderly stages would you ascribe human dignity? Once again, when you begin to negotiate the image of God, you join in a logic of death.

We live not only in the age of megadeath, but we also live in the age of microdeath—death at the microscopic level. We live in the age in which the German medical precept of *Lebensunwerten Lebens*, "life unworthy of life," is being practiced among us. We are now deciding as a society that one life is worthy of life . . . and another life is not. End-of-life decisions are debated, and euthanasia advocates argue in favor of a "good death," which amounts to state allowance for murder.

We live in the age of megadeath and microdeath. We understand that we cannot live in a society like this without sharing in the blood-guilt. We understand that this is represented in the murder statistics of this nation, and we understand that the blood of the innocents cries out. The cold-case files are not only for television dramas. They are to remind us that there will come a day when every sin will be laid bare and every sinner will be made visible, and God's justice will be fully executed.

None of us is safe from the guilt of the Sixth Commandment. The Sixth Commandment points us toward reverence for life, yes, but not for the sake of life itself but because of the Creator. The Sixth Commandment also points us to the need, our desperate need, for the grace and mercy of God shown us in Jesus Christ. He bore in Himself the malice and the hatred and the murderous intention of humanity, and gave His life for sinners, shedding His blood for the remission of our sins.

We read this commandment as Christians. It is addressed to us. Judgment be upon us if we hear it as addressed to someone else.

The SEVENTH COMMANDMENT

You shall not commit adultery.

～ Exodus 20:14

7

Why Adultery Is about Much More Than Sex

a word of confession to those of the female gender. You need to know that we men are not good at the greeting card thing. We are not adept at this for several reasons.

First, it is just hard to bring ourselves to pay that much for painted paper. Second, the words on the card don't match our kind of verbal expression—we just don't talk that way. Part of it is just the sheer embarrassment from realizing that we could never quite say all that florid prose with a straight face.

Still, greeting cards do express something like what men want to express, and we do pay an unconscionable amount of money for this coated paper, which we then give to our loved one.

A few years ago, just days before the event, I realized I was in serious trouble because I was cardless for one of the major occasions of life—Mother's Day. So I quickly went and bought a card. I was successful in bringing home the card, signing the card, and even adding a personal note to my dear wife, Mary. I commented about her sweetness, fidelity, love, giving, and self-sacrifice, not only as my wife but as the mother of our children. I was even successful in remembering where the card was; and so, with great satisfaction (which is another one of the characteristics of the male of the species; when we actually remember to bring the card, there is inordinate self-satisfaction), I presented it to her.

However, as Mary read the card, I noticed that her face did not match my expectation of what her face should betray. So here are two rules of the greeting card thing I learned that day. Rule number one is *remember to get the card*. Rule number two is *read the card* before you give it. That is, read it thoroughly.

In the expression of this greeting card I thanked my wife for so successfully blending together our *two* families—something that heretofore she had not been aware had been done. I had inadvertently chosen a "blended family" card without reading the message.

My *faux pas* has become a part of our family lore. It is a part of my humiliation, and it is a part of my urgent exhortation to other husbands—read the card before you give it!

CARDS FOR ADULTERERS

Greeting cards are a part of our culture, serving as an expression of who we are. Thus, we should take note a new line of cards for adulterers. A few years ago the *Los Angeles Times* reported that Cathy Gallagher developed a line of cards for couples involved in an adulterous affair. The whole idea is profoundly sick, but it tells us a great deal about our society. In an article entitled, "Adulterers Need Cards Too," the writer described a Christmas card developed for this series of greeting cards, which includes this line: "As we each celebrate with our families, I will be thinking of you."

According to the *Los Angeles Times*, Ms. Gallagher says her "Secret Lover" collection of twenty-four cards is the first line exclusively for people having affairs, and she expects, no pun intended, hot sales. According to the *Times*, half of married people have had affairs (though some studies show the figure to be far less).[1] There is a huge market, evidently, in the eyes of those who have produced such cards for their product. Gallagher says her cards express sentiments that people in affairs can't express to anyone else, even their best friends. "These are not sex cards, these are emotional. No other card reflects having to share someone or not being able to be with that person on the holidays." Yes, there is nothing like a little home-wrecking sentiment to warm the adulterer's heart at yuletide.

Ms. Gallagher's line of cards is no threat to the big business of the major greeting card companies, but do not think they are oblivious to those trends. The *Times* contacted Hallmark, the nation's largest greeting card seller, and they said that some of their relationship cards are broad enough that their meaning can vary according to the situation. So, Hallmark does not see a need for an explicit line of cards for adulterers. Spokeswoman Rachel Bolton, explaining the Hallmark Cards line entitled "Between You and Me," said that it covers a wide variety of relationships. For example, she explains the card that says, "I love the private world that you and I share," by saying, "I look at that and I'm thinking of my husband. You might look at that and think of your secretary. The purpose of a greeting card is to make somebody feel good, to solidify or further a relationship."

AN ADULTEROUS GENERATION

We are an adulterous generation. We have institutionalized adultery in our entertainment and in our literature. Adultery is now trivialized by our entertainment culture and routinized by public example. Whatever the genre of literature—mystery, thriller, sci-fi—adultery is expected within the pages. From *Anna Karenina* to *The Bridges of Madison County*, adultery is not only depicted but celebrated. Modern music also has institutionalized adultery through lyrics that celebrate infidelity. At times, adultery creates the dramatic conflict for our sitcoms, and increasingly it is the backdrop to the news stories on the front page.

Adultery **is not only depicted but celebrated.**

A few years ago, I read an interview of one of America's most prolific divorce attorneys. In giving his opinion about the cause of divorce, he said, "Let's get real. I haven't yet had a major divorce in which adultery was not a precipitating cause." Just consider where we are in our culture. In 1850, Nathaniel Hawthorne wrote his most influential novel, *The Scarlet Letter*. The novel depicted a colonial-era America in which adultery was the scarlet sin, and those caught were marked with a scarlet letter and set apart from the society because of their sin. But modern-day America cannot imagine such a sanction—it is virtually a moral impossibility. Instead, we have come to the place where a Generation X spokesman proclaimed, "We are the first generation in which adultery is now not an issue. We have so little expectation of monogamy or of faithfulness, adultery is just no big deal." Gladly, that is not true of his entire generation, but it does seem increasingly true of the culture at large.

This is nothing entirely new, of course, for adultery is not a modern invention. Indeed, the Seventh Commandment reminds us that adultery is one of humanity's first sins. In the first giving of the Ten Commandments in Exodus 20:14, we read these succinct words: "You shall not commit adultery." And adultery was so well understood that it needed no great elaboration, definition, or explanation. We know exactly what God meant here in this commandment. "You shall not commit adultery."

Remember, the Lord gave the Ten Commandments as He was preparing His people to enter the Land of Promise. As they did so, they were to reflect His character, living according to the covenant that He established with them.

In contrast to the expectation of fidelity and faithfulness, the sin of adultery stabbed like a dagger at the very heart of that covenant between God and His people. Today the sin of adultery stabs at the heart of the covenant between a man and a woman—it strikes at the heart of trust and faith, of love and affection. It undermines the husband-wife relationship and the family itself.

A culture that embraces adultery accepts within itself a poison pill for every other relationship.

Adultery begins a breakdown of order that threatens the entire society, for how can we trust each other if we cannot trust each other in our most intimate commitments? If we cannot maintain trust and fidelity within the small and inherently meaningful universe of marriage, how can we trust each other in commerce, in politics, in business, in culture, in life? A culture that embraces adultery, accepts within itself a poison pill for every other relationship, a toxic substance that threatens every other commitment. Adultery is primal in its attack upon all that is honorable and good and true and faithful, unraveling precious bonds and commitments.

In essence, Israel is told, "The other peoples may live by other laws because they are driven by other worldviews and commitments. But you are My people, and you shall not commit adultery." The presence of adultery within the Ten Commandments reminds us of the priority of faithfulness within marriage, and the necessity of keeping that public commitment, living up to vows like, "I will be faithful unto you till death do us part." For God's people, there is to be no adultery, and so the sanction for adultery was death. That most ultimate of sanctions, humanly speaking, was called for because adultery was an attack on the very priority of civilization and society. Marriage is the little universe upon which every other human relationship depends.

And yet we take adultery so casually today, even in many churches. There is little danger of *The Scarlet Letter* being played out in our churches, let alone our culture. Of course, we would have nothing to do with the hypocrisy that Nathaniel Hawthorne described in his novel. However, we must also admit that the contemporary church is so lax in its discipline and so accommodated to sin that even within many congregations there are patterns of adultery known by the congregation and yet unconfronted. Such a congregation accepts within its midst the breaking of a covenant, thus undermining its witness to the covenant of salvation.

SEXUAL ADULTERY: A PICTURE OF SPIRITUAL ADULTERY

Although many within the church fail to comprehend the significance of adultery, any fair reading of the Bible indicates that adultery is not a minor theme. Instead, what we find within Scripture is that the smaller universe of sexual adultery becomes a picture and a paradigm of spiritual adultery. Time and time again, Israel sins against God by playing the harlot—spiritual adultery is identified as its primal sin. Ray Ortlund Jr. brings great scholarly attention to this theme in his book on Israel's adultery, *Whoredom*: "For post-Fall humanity, adulterated by sin, the Bible unfolds the drama of a loving God winning back to himself a pure bride for her one husband."[2]

The biblical theology of adultery is the big story of God's redeeming love, of God's determination to save a people through the blood of His Son for the glory of His name. And note, God saves them *out* of an adulterous generation. It is the Father's pleasure to create a bride for His Son the Bridegroom, and to present this bride to the Bridegroom without spot and without blemish. We in the church of the Lord Jesus Christ look forward to that eschatological promise of the Marriage Supper of the Lamb. God's big purpose of salvation, His dealings with His people, His redeeming love—all these are seen against the backdrop of this biblical theology of adultery.

Why would God choose such an intimate sin in order to demonstrate to us a sin that is so universal? Why does sexual adultery frame the backdrop for the biblical theme of spiritual adultery? The answer is that we can easily understand sexual adultery. When a husband and wife establish a covenant together in marriage, only to have the commitment violated by sexual adultery, the covenant breaker violates the precious and sacred covenant by inviting within the marriage one who does not belong. The adulterer forsakes the one to whom all is due and all must be given, and gives it instead to the one who has no rights to what the adulterer would give.

> *In* spiritual adultery, we forsake our Creator, denying Him His rights.

God provides the picture of sexual adultery in order that we would understand the big picture that spiritual adultery is written large across the Scripture. In spiritual adultery, we forsake our Creator, denying Him His rights. Just as Israel repeatedly violated the covenant in going after other gods, the temptation is always ever so close to us that we would forsake our first love for one another.

Scripture describes Yahweh as a *jealous* God. That word is inherently meaningful within the context of marriage. Like a jealous husband, God will not share Israel with other gods. God will not share Israel's affections and allegiance with pagan deities.

Also, as members of the covenant race of Israel, Israel was forbidden to intermarry, because this is itself a background form of adultery. Think back to Ahab and Jezebel, or Solomon and his many wives and you will see the problem. So, the law itself is written as a gift, given to us that we would know how to live, not only to maximize *our* happiness but to demonstrate God's holiness.

But Israel did play the harlot. In Leviticus 20:4–6, Israel is accused of playing the harlot by seeking false revelation through mediums and spiritists. Israel received warning that anyone who plays the harlot in the worship of Molech must be put to death because this harlotry undermines the very security of the nation. In Numbers 15:38–40,

Israel is accused of playing the harlot through wayward desires and lusts. In Deuteronomy 31:16, Israel is foreseen to play the harlot by experimenting with pagan worship practices, not satisfied with the worship God commands. Israel brought within its own bosom and within its own practice that which was done in the name and for the worship of other gods.

Often in Judges we read of Israel acting as the wayward harlot. In Judges 2:16–17, Israel played the harlot through idolatry, turning their backs on the one true and living God. In Judges 8:27, Israel again plays the harlot in the day of Gideon, incurring God's judgment upon them. And Israel would return again and again to harlotry. In Judges 8:33, we read: "As soon as Gideon died, the people of Israel turned again and whored after the Baals and made Baal-Berith their god."

We understand this subversive reality of adultery.

This theme of spiritual adultery should grab our attention because it describes the day in which we live. We understand this undermining sin, this subversive reality of adultery.

We read the Old Testament and see Israel's continual pulling away from the covenant, their continual turning of their back to God, their continual seduction by other gods, and we wonder how it could happen. How could such things come to be? How could Israel, which was to see itself as having a holy husband Yahweh, make Him a cuckold, shame His name, and deny His glory, by going after other gods?

And then we come to the prophet Hosea, where in a moment of extreme national urgency, God says to Hosea, "Go, take to yourself a wife of harlotry and have children of harlotry; for the land commits flagrant harlotry, forsaking the Lord" (Hosea 1:2 NASB). This drama continues in chapter 2 with a more explicit command:

Contend with your mother, contend, for she is not my wife, and I am not her husband; and let her put away her harlotry from her face and her adultery from between her breasts, or I will strip her naked and expose her as on the day when she was born. I will also make her like a wilderness, make her like desert land and slay her with thirst. Also, I will have no compassion on her children, because they are children of harlotry. For their mother has played the harlot; she who conceived them has acted shamefully. For she said, "I will go after my lovers, who give me my bread and my water, my wool and my flax, my oil and my drink." Therefore, behold, I will hedge up her way with thorns, and I will build a wall against her so that she cannot find her paths. She will pursue her lovers, but will not overtake them; and she will seek them but she will not find them. Then she will say, "I will go back to my first husband, for it was better for me then than now!" (Hosea 2:2–7 NASB)

God exposed the awful nature of idolatry, using the hideous picture of Hosea's adulterous wife. He showed Israel their adulterous practices, illustrating how they had gone whoring after other gods even as this wife went a-whoring after other lovers. The Lord God brought Israel back to Himself through His redeeming love, but in order to do so, He had to pull Israel out of the slimy pit of adultery. Hosea also makes all this very clear in chapter 14:

Return, O Israel, to the Lord your God, for you have stumbled because of your iniquity. Take words with you and return to the Lord. Say to Him, "Take away all iniquity and receive us graciously, that we may present the fruit of our lips. Assyria will not save us, we will not ride on horses, nor will we say again, 'Our god,' to the work of our hands; for in You the orphan finds mercy." (14:1–3 NASB)

What is the redeeming love of God like? The redeeming love of God is so rich that it alone can overcome the hideous reality of adultery. And the wholeness and the healing that comes on the other side of God's redeeming love is such that not only is the sin of adultery forgiven, but the orphan even finds a home. The last verse of the prophet is clear. "Whoever is wise, let him understand these things; whoever is discerning, let him know them. For the ways of the Lord are right, and the righteous will walk in them, but transgressors will stumble in them" (Hosea 14:9 NASB).

ADULTERY IN ISRAEL AND THE CHURCH

The metaphor of sexual adultery to picture spiritual adultery is found in Jeremiah and throughout the prophets. It is in the warp and woof of Scripture, in the very fabric of the biblical revelation. When we turn to the New Testament, we see that the bride and the bridegroom imagery speaks something profound about the church. Now we understand that the covenant people are given an identity, explicitly called the bride of the redeeming Christ.

With adultery seen in all of its evil and grotesque horror, how can the church be aware of the constant danger of spiritual adultery? How are we as unaware as Israel, when we have been made aware of the deductive energy and invitation for the church to abandon its first love, to forsake its bridegroom, and to go a-whoring after other gods?

Yes, let us admit the sad truth—the church also plays the harlot. The church plays the harlot in theology, looking for revelation outside the biblical revelation because she refuses to find satisfaction with what the Scripture teaches. The church plays the harlot by selling out to priorities that are not godly and biblical priorities.

Why would Israel do such a thing? In one sense, it must have been that the invisible Yahweh lost ground continually to the visible pagan idols. As Israel watched the people around them in their worship, they witnessed the manufacturing of idols, the service to the idols—and all this seemed to make sense. It made sense to have a visible pagan god you can set in place and serve. We can forsake the Bridegroom just as Israel forsook Yahweh. It makes human sense in our depravity to want to worship a false god according to its false ways. It is far harder to maintain the fidelity to the god who will not be seen, the one who speaks.

How dare we not observe this in the church—the same temptation, the same pattern, the same whoring, the same grotesqueness, the same effect. New Testament theology teaches us that God is victorious over sin and over death and even over spiritual adultery. God is redeeming a people to the glory of His name, cleansing a people to be presented as a bride—spotless and without blemish to the Bridegroom. God's redeeming love is grace greater than all our sin.

One of the realities of spiritual adultery we must face is that this is not just about other people. We must recognize that when Isaiah says, "All we like sheep have gone astray; we have turned every one to his own way" (Isaiah 53:6), the prophet is speaking about all of us. He is pointing to spiritual adultery on the individual scale as well as on the national and covenantal scale.

Spiritual adultery is not just about other people. The prophet is speaking about all of us.

For Israel, this command had a very clear meaning: So long as there was no sexual activity between a man and a woman, there was no adultery. That does not mean there was no sexual sin, but it does mean that at that point there was no adultery, because adultery comes only as a violation of the marital covenant. Fidelity to covenant was Yahweh's point, a point that the law makes clear. So, in the Old Testament at least, it is simple and clear.

AN ADULTERY UPDATE FROM JESUS

But then, along comes Jesus.

In the Sermon on the Mount, Jesus repeats this commandment, and as is His pattern in this message, He teaches that He came not to abolish the law but to fulfill: "You have heard that it was said, 'You shall not commit adultery.' But I say to you that everyone who looks at a woman with lustful intent has already committed adultery with her in his heart" (Matthew 5:27–28).

In 1976 Jimmy Carter, then the Democratic nominee for president, gave an infamous interview with *Playboy* magazine. During the interview, he made a rather astounding admission. He confessed that he had committed adultery in his heart. This was a concept that the editors of *Playboy* magazine clearly could not understand. Furthermore, in 1976 America, conservative Christians could not believe that Jimmy Carter would survive after granting an interview to *Playboy* magazine. On the other hand, the culture at large could not believe that a serious political candidate could have such hang-ups like this.

Jimmy Carter didn't come up with the idea of committing adultery in his heart. In the Sermon on the Mount, Jesus said adultery is not only a matter of actual sexual sin that involves consummation with a partner. Rather, Jesus raised the bar higher: "I say to you that everyone who looks at a woman with lustful intent has already committed adultery." In essence, Jesus says that to plot and to plan adultery is to commit adultery. In other words, this new covenant is not just about what one does with the body, it is also about what happens in the heart.

Clearly God calls His new covenant people to a standard that is not only about body parts and motion; it is now about the heart and its inclination. Further, we understand that as God's new covenant people, adultery is not a lesser danger, or a lesser temptation. Adultery is an altogether higher, more urgent reality for us. When God presents the bride—His church—without spot and blemish to the Bridegroom, not only will adultery be vanquished, so will lust! At that time, there will be not only no physical breaking of the covenant, there will also be nothing less than full fidelity to the covenant.

Jesus makes clear His expectation for His people. The commandment stands against adultery with our eyes, with our brains, with our imagination. The command is about our attention, the totality of who we are.

So, Jesus sets the bar higher, giving us a heightened standard. You cannot fantasize about this sin. You cannot enjoy the thought of this sin. Jesus says that lust and adultery are the same sin. He did not say lust has the same effect, humanly speaking, as the actual sin of adultery. But He tells us the essence is the same, desiring one who is not deserving of the gift.

SEX AND ADULTERY: A GOSPEL ISSUE

So, Scripture would have us think about adultery in two simultaneous dimensions—spiritual adultery and sexual adultery. Sex is a gospel issue. Paul makes this matter abundantly clear as he writes to the Corinthian church, warning the church not to humiliate its witness. Adultery in our midst undermines our testimony to the gospel of the Lord Jesus Christ. As Paul told the Corinthians, their involvement with sexual sin, and the notorious nature of their sexual practices, undermined their witness to the gospel, making impossible their living together as people of the covenant.

The Seventh Commandment stands against adultery with our eyes and with our passions.

For Christ's people, the sex issue is a gospel issue. Sexual adultery and spiritual adultery go hand in hand. If we take Jesus seriously in the Sermon on the Mount, there are things we must eliminate. We must eliminate pornography. We must eliminate the celebration of sexual sin. We must eliminate the wayward glance. We must eliminate the modern concept of serial monogamy, marriage after marriage after marriage.

Let us be clear. When God said, "You shall not commit adultery," He spoke words Israel could understand. He spoke to something they witnessed and observed in their midst. He spoke of this dagger to the heart of civilization, to the heart of marriage as an institution, and to the heart of Israel's testimony among the nations.

For the church of the Lord Jesus Christ, the urgency is not lesser; it is greater. The tragedy is not minimized; it is maximized, because for God's redeemed people our mission is to both live before the world and to go and take the gospel to the ends of the earth. So, adultery undermines both aspects of that God-given witness.

The Christian ministry is especially undermined by adultery, for the one who assumes a position of authority and responsibility in the church and then commits adultery, not only violates the marital vow, he also undermines the very possibility of effective and faithful Christian ministry. And remember, Jesus said adultery is more than physical; it is also about the mind. We must acknowledge that there are all too many Christian ministers who have not yet committed adultery with the body, but who right now have their ministries undermined because they are committing adultery in the mind and in the heart.

MARRIAGE FAITHFULNESS FOR PASTORS

Let me write to you who would be pastors of the church. You must *establish absolutely unbendable rules for what you will and will not do, where you will and will not go, and with whom you will and will not meet.* In an act of faithfulness to your church and to your Lord, you must never violate those boundaries. In terms of the physical sin of adultery, you can never be alone with a woman. You may think that sounds unrealistic, but I don't care. We are not called to a realistic ministry, but we are called to a holy ministry. You have no business counseling a woman alone. According to the New Testament, you are not even equipped for that. Read Titus. You have no business putting yourself in a position of vulnerability.

Second, as a minister of the gospel, you must *never develop emotional bonds with a person of the other sex who is not your wife.* Far too many men find themselves taking emotional satisfaction in a boost to the ego from a woman who is not their wife, to whom they are not committed, who is not the mother of their children, who does not come to them with demands and expectations, and who does not remind them of their priorities and their commitments. Men have their own egos boosted by a woman drawn to them, thinking the attraction is just because of who they are, their wisdom, or their handsome appearance. When a mutual emotional relationship begins and when the excitement and the anticipation and the enjoyment of that gaze begins, adultery begins.

Third, we must *establish boundaries in our ministry of accountability*. Accountability to our wives is absolutely nonnegotiable. But accountability to the church is also nonnegotiable. In many cases, you will have to teach your church why these boundaries are important. In many cases you are going to have to educate your church through the preaching of the Word and through your urgent exhortation of why these things are important. You must teach your church that the sex issue is a Gospel issue, that they must take those matters seriously before all is lost.

THE BRIDE MADE BEAUTIFUL
THROUGH HIS REDEEMING LOVE

Thinking scripturally, adultery is always a dual focus. Written large across the Scripture is God's redeeming purpose in an adulterated age, in an adulterous generation even like our own, to save a people to the glory of His name. God's redeeming love is demonstrated in that through Christ, God brings to us grace greater than all our sin— even grace greater than the sin we can hardly even imagine in its consequence, importance, grotesqueness, and in its horror—even the sin of adultery.

When the bride is presented to the Bridegroom without spot and without blemish, it will not be because the bride has tidied herself up. It will not be because the bride has decided to cover her own sin. It will not be because the bride, looking back at the horror of what she has done, will simply say, "Well, we will do this no more, and from henceforth we will be faithful." Rather, it is because the redeeming love of God will cleanse this bride of all iniquity. Her sin will be known no more.

In heaven there will be no Ten Commandments. They will not be needed. The glorified church will live out in totality what it means to live to the glory and to the praise of the one true and living God, the *bene Elohim*, gathered before the throne of God. But remember, everyone who is in heaven will be a soul that has at some point committed spiritual adultery. Many who are there, all too many, will be those who have committed sexual adultery.

The church is now instructed to understand the grace and mercy of God in all of its glory over against the honest assessment of this sin in all of its horror. As Joshua reminds us, "Be very careful, therefore, to love the Lord your God" (Joshua 23:11).

The *The* EIGHTH COMMANDMENT

You shall not steal.

～ Exodus 20:15

8

Dealing with the Inner Embezzler

My family and I were visiting the beautiful sun-drenched campus of Stanford University in northern California. As might be expected, I was spending considerable time in the vast bookstore.

My son Christopher, twelve years old at the time, had a particular interest in finding books that I had not seen before, a fairly easy task in the massive university bookstore. Christopher would find books and bring them to me to see if I wanted to purchase them. Then he would go back and find some more.

As I made my purchases and walked outside the bookstore, I noticed that I was without my son. Christopher looked through the windows, saw me, and came running outside the store with a book in his hand, excited to show me his discovery.

All of a sudden, he and I realized that he was on the wrong side of the law. He had left the store without paying for the book. Christopher was petrified. I assured him that we would get him safely back in with the book, and that all would be well. We went back in, and he placed the book on the shelf. But for the remainder of our family trip, whenever we heard a siren, Christopher was certain that it was an all-points bulletin for the boy who had taken the book from the Stanford University bookstore.

HER OWN KITTEN

Childhood experiences inform how we think about even the Ten Commandments. We are taught from earliest age not to steal. We learn the possessive so very quickly: yours, mine, ours, and theirs. However, even as children, we can also understand complicating circumstances. I learned this as a boy, watching and interacting with family members.

My family tells the story of a girl who, as a five-year-old, possessed a desire to have a kitten. One day, she walked into the house with a kitten from the neighbors. She informed her family that the neighbors gave the kitten to her. It was a thrilling turn of events for her. She was a very happy girl—with a kitten.

A couple of years later, a conversation revealed something like this: "That kitten you got, did the neighbors actually give that to you?" She answered no. It turned out that she had decided it was a gift, but she had actually kitten-napped. What made the story very complicated is that those neighbors were thrilled with the theft of this kitten. If you have ever tried to give kittens away, then you can understand the difficulty of this.

I remember being struck by the moral quandary—what do you do with a "hot" kitten, two years after the theft, when the people from whom it was stolen are relieved to know that it was stolen to a good home?

The Eighth Commandment is so simple and straightforward— "You shall not steal"—and the simplicity makes it all the more powerful. The Bible presents a theology of personal possession. One of the temptations in addressing the Eighth Commandment is to go ahead and preach the Tenth Commandment simultaneously. And yet, they are saying the same thing. Both deal with personal property— the eighth forbids stealing and the tenth forbids coveting.

THE DIGNITY OF PERSONAL PROPERTY

Again, there is a covenantal context to these commands. They are addressed to the chosen nation of the people of the covenant, so that Israel would be pleasing unto the Lord and would give an external testimony to the holiness of the God who has made His covenant with Israel. When we take this text within its biblical context and we understand the fullness of a biblical theology of personal possessions, we begin to understand the radical revolution that takes place within the biblical ethic over against the ethic of the peoples of the world, over against the ethic of our natural fallen state, over against all economic theories and all social analysis. The Bible dignifies personal property, and roots this dignity in the *imago Dei*, the image of God. To steal from another is not merely to steal his possession. It is to assault another's dignity as a human being who has the right to the toil of his hands, to the produce of her talents, to the property that is rightfully ours.

This principle is absolutely necessary for the functioning of society. To steal from another is to destroy the societal trust, which is an absolute requisite for a stable economy and stable commerce. Without such trust, there can be no confidence that our neighbors will refrain from stealing our stuff, robbing us not only of our possessions and property, but of our dignity. God warns would-be thieves to respect the rights of property holders and says don't steal their stuff.

THE RIGHT TO PERSONAL PROPERTY

God, through His holy Word, first recognizes a right to personal property. Much of the Old Testament law is given to the regulation of the right of personal possessions and property, so that Israelites would know exactly how to conduct business with one another, and how to respect one another's dignity by respecting one another's property. The Old Testament speaks in great detail about establishing property boundary lines, real estate transactions, weights and measures, business ethics, and laws of inheritance—showing the great concern God had for His people to live righteously with one another in terms of personal economics.

The right to personal property is essential for personal security and for the continuation of family. There is a special connection to the land and to the produce of that land, for just two chapters after the commandment, "You shall not steal," we come across an elaborated set of regulations concerning property rights: "If a man steals an ox or a sheep, and kills it or sells it, he shall repay five oxen for an ox, and four sheep for a sheep" (Exodus 22:1). Just as we saw that murder was treated as an assault upon the dignity of the Creator, so too we understand that taking another's property is an assault upon his dignity as one who was made in the image of God.

The law includes consequences for theft—not unlimited consequences, but expensive penalties nonetheless:

> If a man steals an ox or a sheep, and kills it or sells it, he shall repay five oxen for an ox, and four sheep for a sheep. If a thief is found breaking in and is struck so that he dies, there shall be no bloodguilt for him, but if the sun has risen on him, there shall be bloodguilt for him. He shall surely pay. If he has nothing, then he shall be sold for his theft. If the stolen beast is found alive in his possession, whether it is an ox or a donkey or a sheep, he shall pay double.
>
> If a man causes a field or vineyard to be grazed over, or lets his beast loose and it feeds in another man's field, he shall make restitution from the best in his own field and in his own vineyard.
>
> If fire breaks out and catches in thorns so that the stacked grain or the standing grain or the field is consumed, he who started the fire shall make full restitution.
>
> If a man gives to his neighbor money or goods to keep safe,

and it is stolen from the man's house, then, if the thief is found, he shall pay double. If the thief is not found, the owner of the house shall come near to God to show whether or not he has put his hand to his neighbor's property. For every breach of trust, whether it is for an ox, for a donkey, for a sheep, for a cloak, or for any kind of lost thing, of which one says, "This is it," the case of both parties shall come before God. The one whom God condemns shall pay double to his neighbor. (Exodus 22:1–9)

These laws are especially interesting as we consider the close confinement of Israel's experience, where neighbor lives so close to neighbor, and as we find a tight bond of community. When a coat turns up missing, and it later shows up on someone else, the owner says, "This is it," and if the coat is not returned, the matter goes before the judge. The same process would occur with cattle or lambs, described in detail in verses 10–15:

If a man gives to his neighbor a donkey or an ox or a sheep or any beast to keep safe, and it dies or is injured or is driven away, without anyone seeing it, an oath by the Lord shall be between them both to see whether or not he has put his hand to his neighbor's property. The owner shall accept the oath, and he shall not make restitution. But if it is stolen from him, he shall make restitution to its owner. If it is torn by beasts, let him bring it as evidence. He shall not make restitution for what has been torn.

If a man borrows anything of his neighbor, and it is injured or dies, the owner not being with it, he shall make full restitution. If the owner was with it, he shall not make restitution; if it was hired, it came for its hiring fee.

This is technical stuff. If you wonder how the statutory law of our own civilization builds up so that a lawyer's bookshelf sags with weight, it is on account of all these various types of situations. What happens when an animals dies when no one else is around? What happens when a flame is started and it goes to a neighbor's farm? This is all a matter of property, and it is all derivative of the Eighth Commandment, "You shall not steal."

> *The* dignity of work receives its grounding in creation . . . but takes into account the fall.

Within Scripture, the dignity of work receives its grounding in creation itself, when human beings are told to subdue the earth, to work the earth, and then to enjoy the produce thereof. But we also understand that a biblical theology of work takes into account the fall, when we are told that as a consequence of sin, the earth will no longer yield its fruit so gladly or willingly. Rather, there will be far more toil required in order that the earth will yield its fruit. The cultivation of the land, the tilling of crops, and the entire process of work is now made far more difficult because of the fall, but even that does not remove the dignity of work. Work is itself dignified, and so is the produce of one's hands and the yield of one's investments.

A biblical theology of personal possessions understands the dignity of such possessions, but was it always to be so? Augustine spent many pages and paragraphs contemplating what sex and reproduction would have been like in the Garden of Eden had there been no fall. Others attempt to do the same thing with economics and personal property, asking whether there would be personal property in a world in which there is no sin. We do not know, but we do know that even before the fall, a clear link existed between work and its product.

A biblical theology of personal property turns modern economic theory on its head. The economists do not ground our economic value and our economic agency in creation, in a responsibility to subdue the earth and to link together the toil and the reward, the work and the product. The fall explains human depravity. The fall explains why we must have banks with armed guards, and safes with steel doors and locks, and the Securities and Exchange Commission. Why do we have to have all of these burdensome Internet passwords? It is because we live in a fallen world and there are those who will steal from us. Our moral instincts are now attuned to the fact that some people would steal from us.

When you go to the mall these days and see people get out of their vehicle, what do they do? They click that lock not just once—they click it twice. We have turned into a parking lot of chirping cars. Of course, we also live in a world that doesn't take alarms seriously. When you hear a car alarm going off, you do not assume that a car is being stolen; you assume that a fool has mishandled his car alarm. So, we live in a world in which all these things supposedly make sense. The goal is the protection of personal property—and thus the recognition of human dignity

Scripture puts forth both a positive theology of personal possessions and a negative word of rebuke against stealing. God rebukes the taking of possessions. Strong language is used—God *hates* stealing, robbery, and oppression. Consider the prophets as they thunder against the oppression of the poor and about the business practices of thievery that institutionalize such oppression. If you were to take the Old Testament alone, and collect all the statements whereby God reveals His hatred of those who steal and rob, you would soon realize all those statutes and penalties testify that a crime against property is a crime of great consequence.

Does this emphasis seem somewhat strange to you? I mean, our stuff is just *stuff*. And yet, if we are really honest with one another, we know that it is never just stuff, it is *my* stuff. You've got your stuff, and I've got mine. We borrow other people's stuff with the expectation that we will return it. When we are invited into another person's house, the anticipation is that we will not steal their stuff while there.

Our houses are filled with stuff. We secure our valuable stuff in safe deposit boxes. Most of us have so much stuff we have to build rooms just to hold our stuff. We don't want to part with our stuff, and if we do, it just gives us more room to get other stuff. More than we would ever want to admit, and greater than we would ever want to imagine, we are defined by our stuff: our homes, clothes, books, even our land.

And yet . . . the Bible dignifies all of it by establishing the right to personal property, the right to own what is lawfully ours, the right to the work of our hands, or the yield of wise investment.

In his book *Trust*, Francis Fukuyama convincingly argues that the one single cultural characteristic most requisite of cultural success is trust. He demonstrates that high-trust societies tend to thrive economically, socially, and culturally. But low-trust societies tend to fail. Furthermore, low-trust societies institutionalize thievery.

Russian novelists and prophets explained how this happened during the Soviet years where institutionalized thievery was often the only way you could survive. Taking care of one's family necessitated stealing. One told the story of a factory worker who day after day attempted to steal items from his workplace. Every single day, he took a wheelbarrow filled with factory items, and every day as he left, he got caught. Cylinders, iron ore, tools—his goal was to steal the items in order to sell them for cash for his family. Day after day, the attempted thievery was stopped, and the stuff was taken away from him.

Finally, it came to be his last day at the factory. The commissar was waiting for him to come out with the contraband. He got to the door of the factory, and sure enough, they pulled back the cover from the wheelbarrow and there was stuff. They confiscated it and said to him, "You are a fool! We caught you every single day. You got away with nothing!"

> God warned His covenant people that the toleration of stealing would destroy the nation.

"Sir, Mr. Commissar," he answered, "you are the fool. I have been stealing wheelbarrows."

When you institutionalize thievery, it destroys the trust of the society.

God warned His covenant people that the toleration of stealing would destroy the nation. The prophets thundered against the oppression of the poor, the thievery and cheating and the larceny that would come to represent the nation's covenantal unfaithfulness. Therefore, the one who steals is an enemy of the people of God. This explains, in part, the antipathy to tax collectors by the time of the New Testament and first-century Judaism. Tax collectors institutionalized thievery, and thus the citizens were hated by their own people.

THE REALITY OF THEFT IN THE FALLEN WORLD

Second, God's holy Word describes a fallen world, and we must recognize the reality of thievery in a fallen world.

Martin Luther put it this way: "If we look at mankind in all of its conditions, it is nothing but a vast wide stable full of great thieves."[1] Let me ask you a question. If you leave your house unlocked, or the keys in your car's ignition, or cash out on the table—are you surprised that it is stolen, or are you more surprised in this fallen world that it is not? We know that some people will take from us, and that our possessions are at risk. We live in the midst of a vast wide stable full of great thieves.

Institutionalized thievery is not limited to historical anecdotes from the Soviet Union or from ancient Israel. In our modern context, all the old ways of stealing are still here, and we've invented new ways to steal too. There's securities fraud, estimated to cost the American economy hundreds of millions of dollars—and perhaps billions—a year. There's tax fraud, insurance fraud, Internet fraud, identity theft, plagiarism, copyright violation, unlawful downloading, etc. We can now accomplish theft on a far more massive scale than the ancient Israelites could have ever imagined. With the modern global economy, it is even possible to steal from a great distance, from people we will never see. In a world of billions and trillions of digitalized messages and records, it is getting very difficult and expensive to maintain any kind of adequate security. Thus, we might even be a part of it, unbeknownst to ourselves. We have dirty hands, and we at times conduct our business with dirty dollars.

When looking at the realities of free-market capitalism, we should remember what Winston Churchill said about democracy: "It is the worst form of government, except for all the others."[2] One of the positive aspects of a free-market economy is that it acknowledges the right to personal property and private possessions. It understands that this is not an unlimited right, but nonetheless it is an inherent right; part of life, liberty, the pursuit of happiness, and a part of the dignity of labor— it is one of the requisites for a civilization. A free market economy, more than other systems, tends to link together the risk and reward of investment, toil and reward, work and income. However, it also allows for all kinds of marketing, advertising, and a number of business practices, locally and globally, that call out not the best but the worst.

There is no economic system that does not dirty our hands through complicity with evil.

The Marxists looked at some of the worst evils of free-market economics and sought to alleviate the entire problem by denying a right to private property. In so doing, Marxism denied the personhood of its participants, with inevitably catastrophic results. Like Augustine on sex, it is tempting to imagine what an economy might be like in an unfallen world—but we do not live in an unfallen world. There is no economic system that does not dirty our hands through complicity with evil. There is no economic system that does not create problems even as it solves problems.

How do you achieve something like justice in a world like this?

There is no way to ensure equality of "stuff." You can take everyone's stuff away and you can redistribute all the stuff so that everyone has equal stuff, and just a couple of minutes later it won't be equal anymore. Someone will trade off his stuff for someone else's stuff. Someone will make a better trade, someone will make a worse trade; someone will neglect stuff, someone will simply lose stuff; someone will spend all their stuff, and they'll have no stuff remaining.

That threw the Marxists into ever deeper attempts at achieving some kind of enforced and coercive justice. You think of someone like the late philosopher John Rawls, who said you then must factor into the equation not only what one has, but even one's talent, even one's ambitions, even one's abilities, even one's work ethic, and thus you must equalize all of that. So you have to have a continual reset of stuff, you have to have a continual confiscatory, mandatory, coercive attempt to equalize. This does not work.

In a fallen world, every single economic system entails its own problems.

According to the Scripture, indeed it shouldn't work. You can steal by confiscatory taxations, such that it destroys the rightful link between work and risk, and reward and yield. But at the same time, we have to understand that in a fallen world, every single economic system entails its own problems. If we're really honest, one of the most difficult aspects of any contemporary economic analysis is that we are all deeply complicit in what honestly might be well defined, if not unavoidably defined, as stealing. How do we avoid breaking the Eighth Commandment in a world in which we can walk into a store and see clothing that is available in terms of any sane economic theory at incredibly low prices, and we realize it is because someone somewhere has been paid almost nothing in order to produce this? How do we buy diamonds in a world in which we know that so many diamonds are blood diamonds, bought at the price of human lives?

Very little reward, very little income, very little pay. Are we stealing?

Should we turn the entire equation on its head and say if we were not buying these products those workers would have no income at all? If we were not buying these clothes, they would not have the small income that they are given. Would we say they would have no jobs at all and would simply be thrown back on a subsistence economy? Do we say about the diamonds that if we did not buy these diamonds, there would be no income at all, and the pitiable fragile economy of these depressed nations would simply collapse?

These are questions that defy an easy analysis. The political and economic left is all too hasty in assuming that it knows how to alleviate such injustice, and all too often, those opponents on the right are reluctant to see that there is a problem. In a Genesis 3 world, stealing and robbery and thievery are a lot more complicated than we first might think.

THE ULTIMATE THEFT

Third, the Scriptures tell us that *stealing from God is the ultimate theft*. Summarizing the Ten Commandments into the two tables of the law makes some sense, but it probably misleads more than it suggests the truth. It is not as if you have five commandments addressed toward God, and five commandments addressed toward humanity. All the commands are addressed in terms of our faithfulness to God. God makes claim upon every dimension of our lives, so that our relationships with our fellow human beings are actually a reflection of our relationship with our Creator.

According to Scripture, the ultimate theft is stealing from God. Thus, when we talk about a biblical theology of personal possessions, we have to place that within a biblical concept of stewardship. God's covenant people, the people of the old covenant in Israel, and far more than that, the people of the new covenant in Christ, must recognize that this stuff is simultaneously ours and not ours at all. It is God's and yet entrusted to us. It is ours in some real sense, and yet it is ours to be at the disposal of God's people and God's purposes.

This biblical theology of stewardship is the most revolutionary economic theory of all. It is so radical and so revolutionary that the church hardly seems to understand it, to embrace it, and to live it.

The prophets asked, "Would you rob God?" and our honest answer must be, "Yes, we do." We rob God of the praise due His name. We rob God of the worship that is His proper expectation. We rob God of time and talent that we invest in lesser things. We rob God of possessions and money. We rob God of our priorities and our passions. In all these ways and more, we rob our Creator.

> We rob God of possessions and money. We rob God of our priorities and our passions.

As God's new covenant people in Christ, we must view our wealth not so much as a sign of divine favor, but as a sign of incredible responsibility. It is not enough that we not steal. We must put all that we are and all that we have at the disposal of God, understanding that He ultimately owns all. "For all the earth is mine," He declares (Exodus 19:5). We ultimately must be willing to give all, and as Jesus said so pointedly, to lose all for the sake of the kingdom.

The eighth commandment is so clear and simple, "You shall not steal." Theologian Charles Hodge expressed it well:

This commandment forbids all violations of the rights of property. The right of property as an object, is the right to its exclusive possession and use. The foundation of the right to property is the will of God; by this is meant, one, that God has so constituted man that he desires and needs this right of the exclusive possession and use of certain things. Two, having made man a social being, He has made the right of property essential to the healthful development of society. Three, He has implanted a sense of justice in the nature of man, which condemns as morally wrong everything inconsistent with the right in this position, in this question. Four, He has declared in His Word that any and every violation of this right is sinful. This doctrine of the divine right of property is the only security for the individual or for society. If it be made to rest on any other foundation, it is insecure and unstable. It is only by making property sacred, guarded by the fiery sword of divine justice, that it can be saved from the dangers to which it is everywhere and always exposed.[3]

Hodge is absolutely right. We cannot understand the Eighth Commandment without taking into full consideration every one of the points Hodge made—and yet he did not go far enough. For in reality, we have to recognize that when we read the Eighth Commandment, we read this commandment as thieves. We are robbers, and we steal.

Let us remember that when Jesus was crucified, on His right and on His left were two thieves. The only difference was that one was redeemed and the other was not—and it remains so today.

The NINTH COMMANDMENT

You shall not bear false witness against your neighbor.

~ Exodus 20:16

9

The Truth, The Whole Truth, and Nothing But the Truth

*A*t the seminary I serve, we divide certain areas of responsibility among faculty and administrators. Even country music. All things country—all the "my wife left me and now I can't find my dead dog" songs—I leave these to Dr. Russell Moore and his cultural expertise. But it seems that he is trying to create an intergenerational brain trust on this subject matter by introducing his young boys to the wonders of country music.

Once those two sons wanted to see Willie and Waylon in Luckenbach, Texas. Somehow they fixated on this, and one of them asked their father, "Daddy, when we're six, all grown up, mature men of the world, can we go to Luckenbach, Texas?"

"Yes!" Dr. Moore said.

At the time, they were nowhere near six, but they soon were, and they were packing their bags for Luckenbach, Texas.

Now, there is very little reason to take two young boys to

Luckenbach, Texas, other than the fact that one promised to take them there. Someone suggested that Dr. Moore simply ought to take them to Dallas and tell them it is Luckenbach, Texas—a plan of action which I am quite sure our senior vice president for academic administration would not choose. But I could tell there was a glint in my colleague's eye as he reflected on how the "Dallas plan" might be a way out of this conundrum of figuring out what to do with two six-year-olds in Luckenbach, Texas.

We have all been there. We recognize the convenience of the lie, and what often appears to be the inconvenience of the truth. For reasons that seem sensical to us, the lie can be far more attractive than the truth. We learn very early in life to lie, and we become accustomed to speaking and to hearing lies. We know that some people lie even when the truth would serve them better. We assume and consume lies. We even believe the lies of advertising—"Buy this product and you will be satisfied," or "Buy this therapy, and you will be whole." But lies are deadly. They flatter and seduce, deceive and delude, kill and destroy.

> We assume and consume lies. They deceive and delude, kill and destroy.

Then, along comes the Ninth Commandment, stating very simply, "You shall not bear false witness against your neighbor"—just a few words that at face value seem to make perfect sense. We are told from the cradle that this means no lies. Yet as children we were always having stories read to us that weren't true; I never believed that Horton really heard a Who. And there can be childhood confusion when we use a euphemism, such as "telling a story," for the word *lie*. Eventually children figure out what it means for a story to be an ugly lie, to be a false witness against one's neighbor or against one's God.

John Calvin explained that as the Eighth Commandment, "You shall not steal," tied his hands, so the Ninth Commandment tied his tongue. In this sense, we are all now tongue-tied. Humanity is filled with connoisseurs of lies, and then along comes the commandment that "You shall not bear false witness against your neighbor."

Here we have the law given by the Creator to the covenant people of Israel. This is the law that was written by God upon the heart and writ large throughout creation, but in the specific form of these Ten Words, it is given as a gift to the covenant people of Israel. As these ten commands begin to draw to a close, Israel hears that one of the chief hierarchical concerns of a holy God is that His people will not bear false witness against one another.

THE POWER OF A LIE

A lie can forfeit a life, or destroy a reputation. The specific first reference of this text is to a court of law—to the law as lived out, as judgments were made in the courts. Every single day, individual Israelites gave testimony through the legal process. In an honor culture, where reputation meant everything and where life and death could hang in the balance, false witness could kill. The law of Israel included a detailed system for how evidence or witnesses could be brought against someone, especially those accused of a very serious crime. It is no surprise, then, that the Old Testament repetitively prohibits false witness. Truth must always be spoken about one's neighbor, for even one incident of false accusation could unravel the social fabric of an entire community.

Lies subvert a fundamental requirement for civilization—trust. If we do not trust our neighbors to speak the truth, then ultimately no civilization is possible. If we cannot trust the courts to get a true witness and to eliminate a false witness, then the courts become a sham and justice becomes an illusion. If we believe the courts can be manipulated, then there is no foundation of trust for society. False witness against neighbor would threaten Israel's testimony even as it diminished their testimony to the nations.

CLEAR INSTRUCTIONS ON SPEAKING THE TRUTH

Consider how many texts in Scripture deal with false witness and lying. Zechariah 8:16 reads, "Speak the truth to one another; render in your gates judgments that are true and make for peace." Third John 12 states, "Demetrius has received a good testimony from everyone, and from the truth itself. We also add our testimony, and you know that our testimony is true." In Proverbs 31:8–9, we find the duty to stand for truth as a matter of heart conviction: "Open your mouth for the speechless, in the cause of all who are appointed to die. Open your mouth, judge righteously, and plead the cause of the poor and needy" (NKJV). In Leviticus 19, a chapter dealing with our responsibility to our neighbor, we read in verse 15, "You shall do no injustice in judgment. You shall not be partial to the poor, nor honor the person of the mighty. In righteousness you shall judge your neighbor" (NKJV). In similar fashion, Proverbs 14:5 says, "A faithful witness does not lie, but a false witness breathes out lies." Here is the concern in Scripture that a false witness can lead to a capital execution, or conversely, could allow the guilty to go free. "A truthful witness saves lives, but one who breathes out lies is deceitful" (Proverbs 14:25). The contrast is clear—lying kills, but truth delivers souls.

According to the apostle Paul, we are to tell the truth at all times—we owe one another the truth. Thus he asked the Corinthian believers, "Do I make my plans according to the flesh, ready to say 'Yes, yes' and 'No, no' at the same time? As surely as God is faithful, our word to you has not been Yes and No" (2 Corinthians 1:17–18).

We owe one another an unvarnished answer, Paul explained. Our yes is to be yes, our no is to be no—the two should not be confused.

We are not to bear false witness, first of all, in the court of law. If we are drawn into litigation or into the judicial process, we are to bear true witness. But secondly, truth telling is extended beyond that, even in our casual conversation, in our social interaction, in our e-mails, and in our preaching. This is not just about when we have to stand up in court and "swear to tell the truth, the whole truth, and nothing but the truth." We have an absolute moral obligation to speak the truth in all our private conversations and in every communication.

THE GOD OF TRUTH

Our need to speak the truth is rooted in God's own character. The God who created us, who established His covenant with Israel, and who redeemed His people through the blood of His Son—He is the God of all truth. He Himself *is* truth. All that He does, all that He says, all that He reveals, all the acts He performs, are words and deeds and acts of *truth*. In His High Priestly prayer, Jesus asked the Father to, "sanctify them [that is, His own] in the truth; your word is truth" (John 17:17).

Everything about God reflects absolute and undiluted truth. In Him there is no lie. His justice and His righteousness are established in an absolute veracity, in absolute truth. He hates lies, and His followers must be a people of truth. His creatures are obligated to the truth.

The Son of God, Jesus Christ, says, "I am . . . the truth" (John 14:6). Conversely, we are told that Satan is "the father of lies" (John 8:44). We are told in the New Testament that the church, the people of God, is to be the people of the truth. Christians are to have within ourselves the Spirit of truth, but we are warned about deceiving spirits among us.

The entire biblical worldview takes excruciating seriousness in noting the difference between the true and the false, even as the distinction between the holiness of God and our human sinfulness is infinite. The difference between the lie and the truth points to the ugliness and deadliness of sin.

CALLED TO BE PEOPLE OF TRUTH

We fall so tragically short of the glory of God. We say we worship and follow God, and yet we lie. It is so important to tell the truth, because ultimately truth is about God and His own character. If God's people do not reflect His own concern for the difference between the truth and a lie, then we sin and create a scandal to the gospel. Ultimately, speaking the truth is connected to our worship of God and our following Jesus—we show whether we love the truth and hate the lie.

Telling the truth is first of all about God and His character. But secondly, it is also about our fellow human creatures. We owe the truth to everyone—to every single fellow image bearer of God.

In a fallen world, lies come in a variety of forms: big and small, crude and sophisticated, slick and awkward, long and short, quiet and loud lies. There is propaganda, where the bigger the lie, the more readily it is believed. There are huge lies of ideology. There are little intimate lies within relationships. The fact is, a lying tongue can adapt to meet any situation in which it finds itself.

DOES TRUTH EXIST?

There are some who say truth doesn't matter anymore, because truth doesn't even exist. The very act of making a distinction between the truth and a lie assumes a worldview that has been forfeited by many in our postmodern society. Our prevailing society denies the existence of absolute or universal truth. It argues that all truth is socially constructed—truth is simply a compliment we pay to propositions that serve our interests. We call such propositions true, because if we establish them as true and bind them as authority on others, then we can extend our own power. All our talk about truth is only a social construction for the oppression and manipulation of others, many argue. Indeed, this is one of the major tenets of academic postmodernism. The late philosopher Richard Rorty distilled this postmodern concept down to its very essence, when he said, "Truth is made, not found."

Truth is *made*. Let us flesh out this postmodern argument. If truth is a social construction, then we create the truth as we go along. It is not really true if it is just what we *call* true. Postmodernism breaks truth down into different cultural linguistic systems and different systems of power and oppression, so there are different truths for different people, for different places, for different needs, for different purposes, for different manipulations. In the end, there is no distinction between the truth and the lie, and in this brave new postmodern world we are supposed to understand that belief in truth is a luxury we can no longer afford.

Such is the postmodern mind. It is the denial of any responsibility to tell truth to one another . . . the denial that truth even exists. Friedrich Nietzsche wrote this about truth:

> What then is truth? A moveable host of metaphors, metonymies, and anthropomorphisms, in short, a sum of human relations which have been poetically and rhetorically intensified, transferred and embellished, and which after long usage, seem to a people to be fixed, canonical and binding. Truths are illusions which we have forgotten are illusions. They are metaphors that have become worn out and have been drained of sensuous force, coins which have lost their embossing and are now considered as metal and are no longer as coins.[1]

That is a devastating piece of writing. Those words represent the fall of an entire civilization. This means the collapse of any shared meaning. Nietzsche's words are a denial of any responsibility of truth one to the other, a denial that truth even exists. Here we see nihilism in its unvarnished, uncut face. The title of Nietzsche's essay, "On Truth and Lies in a Nonmoral Sense," betrays the entire collapse, for how in the world can you have a conversation about truth and lies in a *nonmoral* sense? This can only work if you believe there is no morality, and no such thing as a lie.

"The truth," Nietzsche says, is simply a "sum of human relations which have been poetically and rhetorically intensified, transferred and embellished, and which after long usage, seem to a people to be fixed." Let us be real clear about this. If that is true, then we are closing up shop because there is no reason to believe in God—and that *is* the truth. Poetically fixed, culturally reinforced truth claims—that is all there is? If there is no truth, there are no lies. If there is no truth, there is no God. If there is no lie, there is no sin. If there is no sin, there is no Gospel—it is all a lie.

However, you cannot really talk about lies and truth in a non-moral sense, even if you are Nietzsche, because you have to eventually say that claiming something false as true is a lie. And if claiming something false as true is a lie, then there is some independent judgment. We do know that truth does exist, and that knowledge is essential to humanity. We are trapped within the knowledge that God has placed within us, the conscience that is the structure of our own mental operation and the structure of morality in the world beyond. We can deny there is a truth, but we then have to defend the truthfulness of the claim that there is no truth.

That is why postmodernism collapses in upon itself. This explains why there are no postmodernists in airplanes at 33,000 feet—no one wants gravity to be socially constructed. No one wants a postmodern heart surgeon, snipping arteries here and there according to personal preference. No one wants a postmodern banker. You want your banker to believe that two plus two equals four when it comes to your dollars. But we live in the culture of the lie, where many people believe the lie that there is no difference between truth and the lie. And the pedigree of the modern philosophical subversion of truth goes back further than Nietzsche. Immanuel Kant's critical philosophy and epistemology left doubt as to whether human beings can ever really know the truth at all.

> *No* one wants a postmodern heart surgeon, snipping arteries here and there according to personal preference.

In popular culture, we live in an age in which people think they can improve upon the truth. Historian Edmund Morris was commissioned to write what was supposed to be the great biography of Ronald Reagan. Those of us who had read Morris's biography on Theodore Roosevelt waited with high anticipation for this great biography of Ronald Reagan. Morris titled the book *Dutch*, and that made sense because that was Reagan's nickname. The book displayed Reagan's photograph on the front, and that too made sense. But when the book was released, Edmund Morris made an incredible admission. He said that the book actually wasn't intended to be a traditional biography. Rather, it is traditional biography mixed with his own fictional imagination. The publisher of the book even had the audacity to say this is an improvement upon the biographical form.

Edmund Morris, my mother would say, is telling a story. The problem is, the book is absolutely useless, because there is no distinction between the truth and a lie. And in this case, the lie is his own imaginative and fictive recreation of events and conversations. Thus, you cannot trust it. It is absolutely audacious for the publisher to suggest that this is an improvement in the biographical genre, but this tells us a great deal about our age.

More recently, James Frey's autobiographical book, *A Million Little Pieces*, came out, leaving his reputation later in a million little pieces itself. It turned out that all the awful and excruciating experiences about which he wrote he had not actually experienced.

Some doubt that it is now even possible to lie. Others argue that it could be healthy to lie.

Although he wrote in the genre of personal memoir, it turned out that it wasn't. Oprah Winfrey loved the book, made it one of her Book-of-the-Month selections, and had Frey on her program. But when the lie was revealed, and the book was exposed as a fabricated autobiography, Oprah had him back on her program and confronted the author with his lies. He admitted to a series of altered facts and was largely discredited.

But two years later Frey told a reporter for *USA Today*, "I wanted to play with the idea of what is fiction and what is nonfiction. I don't think the label is important. It's all manipulated material. . . . What is important to me is making a connection with the readers. That they feel something."[2]

Some doubt that it is now even possible to lie. Others argue that it could be healthy to lie. A magazine entitled *Child* published an article, "The Truth about Lying"—which by its title sounded promising. But the caption underneath the title said this:

> The old view: Lying, like other issues of other morality, was seen only in black and white. Children were taught that all lying was bad and deserving of strict punishment and frequently reminded that lying will make your nose grow as long as Pinocchio's. New view: Today, some lying is considered normal. In fact, a child's first few lies are seen as an important step in the development of the self.[3]

A culture that encourages parents to see their children's lies as "an important step in the development of the self" is a culture of institutionalized dishonesty. Our calling as parents is to teach our children to be those who tell the truth—and require our children to be truth tellers. Society itself depends upon a request for and a commitment to the truth. Of course, in a fallen world we know that some people will lie, and thus we have a criminal code that includes perjury.

The proposal that parents see lies as developmental tools is just one more symptom of the therapeutic worldview, in which we just assume that lying serves the interests of our personal development, so we help our children develop into liars.

THE PEOPLE OF TRUTH

However, as the people of the truth, Christians have a twofold, God-assigned responsibility to speak what is true and also to speak on behalf of truth itself. There is a duality to our responsibility, a missiological and evangelistic responsibility in this postmodern age. We sometimes have to look to people and say, "What I'm telling you is true, and by the way, I mean by that that it really is true!"

This is not new. As far back as the 1970s, Francis Schaeffer was telling people about the difference between truth and *true truth*. As he saw then, our Christian responsibility is to tell the truth—and to tell the truth *about the truth*.

It is a mark of the Christian to be truthful, for Christianity is established in God's truth. God's people, formed into local congregations, are like islands of truth in the midst of an ocean of lies. God's people are to be the communities of truth—the people of truth.

There is an inner logic to the Ten Commandments that is often missed. We tend to remember the commandments as disconnected and self-contained. Actually, the commandments are a whole, intended by God to be heard and obeyed together. Taken as a whole, these commandments frame the identity of God's covenant people.

Consider the Third Commandment: "You shall not take the name of the Lord your God in vain, for the Lord will not hold him guiltless who takes His name in vain." The inner logic of the Ten Commandments becomes clear when we understand that this means we are not to bear false witness about God. The commandment is clear: do not take God's name in vain; do not bear false witness against the Creator and tell lies about Him.

The worst possible lie we can tell is a lie about God. Getting theology wrong ... is to lie about God.

Now, when we come to the Ninth Commandment, we are instructed that we are not to bear false witness against another human being. To bear false witness against God is to commit idolatry. To bear false witness against our neighbor is to do violence against him.

The worst possible lie we can tell is a lie about God. Long before we get to a concern for truthfulness among human creatures, God directs us to the imperative of truthfulness concerning Himself. The reputation for which we must be most concerned is the reputation of God Himself. Theology is speech. Doctrine is speech. The danger of getting doctrine and theology wrong is not merely to come up short on a systematic theology exam. Getting theology wrong is to bear false witness about God. It is to lie about God. It is to create an idol in the place of the one true and living God.

Luther became convinced that the chief violators of the Ninth Commandment are heretics and false prophets and empty preachers. I wonder how many preachers, in their sermon preparation, worry about breaking the Ninth Commandment (bearing false witness against God), as well as the Third Commandment (taking the Lord's name in vain).

In Jeremiah 14:14, the Lord said to Jeremiah, "The prophets are prophesying lies in my name. I did not send them, nor did I command them or speak to them. They are prophesying to you a lying vision, worthless divination, and the deceit of their own minds."

In Isaiah 44, a classic chapter about idolatry, the delusional man of idolatry cuts down a tree, using one half to make his fire and the other half to make his idol (verses 13–17). The lie of idolatry deceives him to the extent that he has not the wisdom to say, "Is there not a lie in my right hand?" (verse 20).

TELLING THE TRUTH ABOUT GOD

You see, theology is not just about orthodoxy and heterodoxy, right and wrong, or accuracy and inaccuracy. Theology is about the truth and a lie. In Romans 1, Paul tells us that in our sinfulness, we exchange the truth of God for a lie. Heresy is here redefined as a lie—a lie about God.

What an awful thought, and yet, how frequently is it done. Far too many preachers pour forth theological lies like, "Don't worry, God just wants you to be happy." Heresy might be the clearest example of a lie that leads to death—an eternal death. We dare not bear false witness about God. We dare not take refuge in ambiguity.

Dr. James P. Boyce, the founder of the seminary I serve, gave an important address in 1856 that became the Magna Carta for the institution.[4] He spoke about the professional responsibility of the faculty, saying that all who teach here must sign the confession of faith, pledging to teach in accordance with and not contrary to all that is contained therein. But he did not stop there. He went on and said that the faculty member must sign "without hesitation or mental reservation." This makes the expectation and requirement clear.

Augustine understood the concept of mental reservation when he talked about how we can lie by appearing to say something that is partly true.[5] We can lie, reserving to ourselves the knowledge that we do not mean what we say—thus a mental reservation. But there must be no crossed fingers behind our back.

This serves to remind us of our continual dependence upon Scripture, for how else are we going to speak the truth about God unless we are utterly dependent upon His truthful revelation of Himself? If we ever depart from this truthful revelation, either by heresy or by vain imagination, we transform the truth into a lie and we lie about God. We must trust the Scriptures.

TELLING THE TRUTH TO ONE ANOTHER

As we move from the Third Commandment to the ninth, we confront a very real responsibility to our Creator, which leads to our responsibility to our fellow creatures. What we owe to God leads inexorably to what we owe to each other. In the original context of Exodus 20:16, when we read, "You shall not bear false witness against your neighbor," this was interpreted by Israel to mean, "Don't lie to a fellow child of Israel. You do not lie to a fellow member of the covenant community." Again, in Leviticus 19, we see that the neighbor is the one who is near to you, your kin, and your fellow covenant keeper. And so, the covenantal responsibility forbade lying and commanded truth.

But we are not left there. As Christ's people, we must move into the question, "But who is my neighbor?" And the answer we receive is that our neighbor is no longer just our family and the familiar, it is no longer just our tribe and town, and it is no longer just the covenant people of God. In the parable of the Good Samaritan, we discover that everyone is our neighbor, and thus we owe the truth to everyone. What did Jesus say? "You shall love the Lord your God with all your heart and with all your soul and with all your mind. This is the great and first commandment. And a second is like it: You shall love your neighbor as yourself. On these two commandments hang all the Law and the Prophets" (Matthew 22:37–40). In telling the truth rather than bearing false witness, the love of God and love of neighbor are combined together in one commandment. The key to understanding this is that our neighbor is God's creature.

Now we must never act as if all this is always an easy matter. Back in 1803, the Long Run Baptist Church in Louisville, Kentucky, had a church fight and split apart. There was theological debate over the issue of lying. The question was, if an Indian raiding party comes and demands of you to tell them where you have hidden your children, are you obligated to tell them the truth or are you allowed to tell them the lie? This was not an abstract question in 1803, and it led to a split within the congregation. And they split into the lying Baptists and the nonlying Baptists, or so they would at least fancy themselves. At least we can admit that lying is an issue worth splitting over.

WHAT ABOUT DECEPTION?

Indeed, this is an old question. What about the Hebrew midwives? What about Rahab the harlot (Joshua 2)? Augustine said, when forced into such a situation, one should respond with silence. Certainly, the Bible depicts deception. In fact, God actually commands deception at some points. In Joshua 8:1 and 2 Samuel 5:22 God commands Israel in its military operations to deceive.

You can lie in more than one way. As theologian Charles Hodge said, you lie by leaving the lights on in your home as if you are there so that no robber will enter. By the way, Hodge said that is an advisable lie. In other words, it is not the kind of lie envisioned by the Ninth Commandment.

As Winston Churchill said to Joseph Stalin in the midst of World War II, "Truth is so precious that she should always be attended by a bodyguard of lies."[6] In a purely secular context, Churchill means that deception in war is a necessity.

So, how do we put all that together? Well, this is no easy question. There is always the danger that we will deceive ourselves and grow comfortable with the lie. There is always the potential that we will rationalize our way into lying once again. We do understand that there are excruciating situations, and even ministers face excruciating situations. When an elderly man is facing his last days, do you tell him just how awful his physical predicament is? Does the doctor always owe the patient the absolute truth? Or, if that is settled as a matter of medical ethics, do family members owe each other the truth in that situation? When an elderly woman asks the one who is with her, "Am I still beautiful?" how are you going to answer? That one is easier than it sounds, for the answer is always yes because a fellow human made in the image of God is beautiful. But perhaps she is asking in a different sense.

We find ourselves repeatedly in situations where it appears that the lie will serve better than the truth. We do know this: God will judge the lie, and we will be judged for our lies. We also know this: Lies hurt, lies kill, lies deceive, and lies destroy. Finally, we know

When an elderly woman asks the one who is with her, "Am I still beautiful?" how are you going to answer?

this: We owe the truth to God, and because we owe the truth to God we owe the truth to each other and to all others.

HOW TO RECOGNIZE THE TRUTH

T. S. Eliot said humankind cannot bear much reality. In other words, we can't bear the truth. That is an awful indictment, isn't it? And yet, Jesus says in John 8:32, "And you will know the truth, and the truth will set you free." Let's admit that the only reason we know the difference between the truth and a lie is because we know the one true and living God. Let's admit that the only way we know what it means to tell the truth is because we have received the truth. And let's admit to each other that the only way we recognize the truth as the truth is because the Holy Spirit opened our eyes to see the truth.

Alone, not only would we not bear much reality; we would not even see the reality. But by God's grace, we have seen the truth. We have come to know the One who is the way and the truth and the life.

Thus we have been incorporated by the power of God into the people of truth, and even and especially in the midst of this postmodern age, we are to be the people of the truth—people who speak the truth and only the truth. We're to be the people who speak up for the truth.

TO HONOR AND TELL THE TRUTH

"You shall not bear false witness against your neighbor." You know, we all know what we're told in the beginning. This means do not lie. But of course it means far more than that. It means you tell the truth.

It is certainly not an accident that the word we use so often for *evangelism* is the word *witness*. Remember, not only do we owe unto each other the truth and not the lie, but the apostle Paul tells us we owe to all people everywhere the gospel of Christ, to be not only a nonlying witness, but to be a gospel witness. "You shall not bear false *witness* against your neighbor." "You will be my *witnesses* in Jerusalem and in all Judea and Samaria, and to the end of the earth" (Acts 1:8).

God's people are a people of the truth. We are to honor and tell the truth, to defend and discern the truth, to love the Bible as the Word of God that is truth without any mixture of error, and to stand for the truth. We are to uphold the truth, even if the whole world disbelieves, hates, and subverts the truth. We are the people of the truth for one single and irreducible reason—our God is true.

The TENTH COMMANDMENT

You shall not covet your neighbor's house; you shall not covet your neighbor's wife, or his male servant, or his female servant, or his ox, or his donkey, or anything that is your neighbor's.

～ Exodus 20:17

10

Why Covetousness Kills Contentment

*E*very family has its rules. Every school, whether elementary or college, begins with understanding the rules. Every institution has its rules. When you join the Boy Scouts or Girl Scouts, you get a list of rules.

We are accustomed to lists of rules. In elementary school they go like this: everyone has to follow the leader, everyone has to walk quietly in line, everyone sits in his own desk. In Boy Scouts, you can't go swimming without a buddy. Teenagers want to drive but must wait to get their learner's permit until they show that they know the rules of the road. They may not yet know anything about the feel of a steering wheel or how the braking system works, but they first learn the rules, the laws that govern the road. So they learn what the yellow line means, what the double yellow line means, what the stop sign means, and what all the signals mean.

Whether at undergraduate or graduate school, college students first receive an informative handbook, and the handbook includes rules. There are, it seems, a minimal number of principles and rules that are absolutely necessary to regulate academic life together. Without them, students would be left with chaos and subjectivity and incivility and worse.

Every arena of life comes with its own set of rules. By the inclination of our fallen hearts, we come to expect a rule-based culture.

A part of what makes a rule-based culture very comfortable for us is that we feel we are doing fine so long as we are inside the rules. If we can just see the list and understand that we do not break these rules, we think that we are at peace and all is well with our souls. It is a lie, of course, because the rules can't save us.

IF WE BREAK JUST ONE RULE

When we come to the Ten Commandments, we are not merely looking at ten rules. They do regulate, they certainly are rules, but they go far beyond rule. This is God's *law*—divine revelation and divine command. And yet, it is easy to read these commands and think, *Well I don't break that one, and I don't break this one, so I must be fine.* It is an illusion, it is a lie, and it is wrong. What is more, this kind of thinking does not work when you get to the Tenth Commandment. When we come to this, the final of our Ten Words, we find a commandment that we all must admit we have broken, are perhaps now breaking, and will probably break in the future.

The Tenth Commandment declares: "You shall not covet your neighbor's house, you shall not covet your neighbor's wife, or his male servant, or his female servant, or his ox, or his donkey, or anything that is your neighbor's"(Exodus 20:17). This is the first and only commandment that directly addresses itself to the internal life, reaching the intention of the heart. Similar to the Sermon on the Mount, this command addresses not only what we do but even gets to the heart of our desires and wants. Unlike a schoolteacher, scoutmaster, or parent who could read our behavior but not our mind, God—the One who gave us this law—reads our heart and soul. He knows our covetousness.

"You shall not covet." Even the word itself is strange to our modern ears. Does the moral vocabulary of our culture even include the word *covet*? In the process of raising children, do parents use this word? Unless we utilize a catechism or are specifically going through the Ten Commandments, it is unlikely that *covet* is a word we would choose to use. We might use *jealousy* or *envy*—and these are included in covetousness.

Even as it is a strange word to modern ears, this is an indispensable command because the Ten Commandments are a symphonic whole. The law is not merely divisible into ten different principles or commands or moral instructions, but is a comprehensive whole, given for our good. The commandments are addressed to us so that we will know what a covenant-keeping God requires of His people. They reveal the covenantal love and expectation of God. This is a word from the Rescuer to the rescued, from the Lord to His people. Here we see what God our Sovereign knows is good for us.

The Ten Commandments reveal both instruction and information. We desperately need to know what it means to covet and why there is sickness and death in coveting. We need to know why coveting is so seductive that we give ourselves over to it.

There is sickness and death in coveting.

The First Commandment and the Tenth Commandment are like bookends to make the symphonic comprehensiveness of the Decalogue clear. Even as the First Commandment—"You shall have no other gods before me" (Exodus 20:3)—underlies all of the other commandments, so also when we reach the Tenth Commandment we reach the one that helps to explain all of the other commandments in retrospect.

Remember, because the Ten Commandments begin with monotheism and the total claim of a God upon His people, the end point is not merely the external directive addressed to our actions. Rather, the final commandment deals with our desire. And that word *desire* infuses our understanding of the entire Decalogue, because at the heart of all the commandments is the desire we have for our own personal preferences. We desire our own personal, private God—to have the god we would create rather than the God who created us. We desire what belongs to His name and His name alone. We would have His authority and His rights for ourselves. We desire autonomy rather than to honor our parents. We desire our neighbor's possessions, spouse, life, and reputation—a seemingly unquenchable desire.

This commandment warns us twice, "You shall not covet," and there is unusual specificity here that fits the situation of God's covenant people Israel, from "your neighbor's wife" to your neighbor's "ox or his donkey." Reading this with twenty-first-century eyes, we can probably state with honesty that we have not coveted our neighbor's ox or his donkey. But we have coveted a neighbor's Lexus, plush lawn, clothes, athletic ability, or his social status. Covetousness seems to get right to the marrow of our bones.

The double negation—"You shall not . . . you shall not"—is without parallel in the Ten Commandments, and for this reason some count the commandments differently, finding two separate commandments here. I believe the Reformation structure of counting the commandments is correct, and that what we have here in verse 17 is one comprehensive commandment. It really gets right after the very root of what it means to covet, which is to desire that which is wrong to desire and to want that which it is wrong to want.

TO COVET: "TO HANKER AFTER"

Several scholars suggest that this word is difficult to match in terms of an English analogy, and perhaps the best way to put it is that coveting means "to hanker after." Although I'm sure you don't use that term every day, perhaps it does communicate. We are a hankering people. We hanker after things, and we live in a society that thinks we ought to be hankering even more. Just look at the advertising and watch the images that come before our eyes. We are told that you are what you own, what you buy, what you wear, what you drive, and what you want.

Sometimes I get the opportunity to speak in remarkable academic settings—at very elite universities and institutions—and you can almost taste in the air the promise that you are your degree, you are your alma mater, you are all that elite education embodies. This spirit whispers in your ear, saying, "This is who you are, and you should desire to be here. You should make this the focus of your desire, and if you do come here, then when you graduate, all these other things will come unto you as well—the Lexus and the Mercedes, the prestigious law firm or the profitable medical practice, the cultural accolades, the *Who's Who*, etc." We are a hankering people.

The problem is, we hanker after the wrong things. "You shall not covet," is more emphatic, lengthy, and detailed than the other commandments, because there is a particular seduction to this whole sin of coveting. It must be that we would blind ourselves to this particular sin quite naturally. We could hardly blind ourselves to the fact that we've committed murder, adultery, or that we have dishonored our parents or built an idol. But this commandment against coveting reaches to the interior of the heart, and we have the capacity as fallen human creatures to lie to ourselves about what we're doing. Thus, this last commandment comes with this double negation and with this much specificity.

Coveting affects those who otherwise look morally upright, even those who preach and teach the Word.

Martin Luther said that this last commandment is addressed not to those whom the world considers wicked rogues, but precisely to the most upright, to people who want to be commended as honest and virtuous because they have not offended against previous commandments. The seductive power of coveting is that it affects those who otherwise look morally upright, those who go to church, those who preach and teach the Word. Coveting is so insidious. Luther added that we know how to put up a fine front to conceal our rascality.[1] Or, as nineteenth-century English Baptist Andrew Fuller said, "It has long appeared to me that this species of covetousness will in all probability prove the eternal overthrow of more characters among professing people than almost any other sin. And this because it is almost the only sin which may be indulged in a professor of religion and at the same time supported."[2]

We read the Ten Commandments, we hear the Ten Commandments, we receive the Ten Commandments, and if we are not painstakingly honest, we will delude ourselves into thinking that we keep the commandments. But when we get to coveting, we realize that we are not only nailed, we are caught in the very act. It is like the indictment that comes down in the middle of the performance of the crime. And it is the case that we are men and women in motion; the motion of coveting.

We must also consider the deceitfulness of riches. Clearly, there is a materialistic aspect to this tenth commandment. After all, the warning is about coveting a neighbor's house, his wife, his male or female servant, his ox, his donkey, anything that belongs to your neighbor. Jesus told the parable of the sower and the soils, speaking of the thorny, weed-infested ground in which the good seed of the gospel appears to take root but is eventually strangled out by the thorns. It never bears fruit, a condition Jesus condemns. So, what does Jesus describe as the problem? What is the weed that infests this garden? The weed is "the deceitfulness of riches," a constant biblical theme (e.g., Matthew 13:22).

This big lie is that we are what we own, or we can be what we want to own, what we wear, or what we drive. What do we do when we get a new car? We have got to show it to someone, almost like there is no fun to be had if nobody is around to covet it. We provide a drive-by opportunity to covet. Those things we covet—we are experts when it comes to these.

POSSESSIONS, CONSUMERISM, AND COVETING

Do you remember the television program *Lifestyles of the Rich and Famous*? In addition to the obnoxious host, what was truly odd about the program is that you never actually saw anyone rich or famous. You saw their home, cars, yacht, and their stuff, and that was evidently enough because you would not actually see the owner. You just had to take Robin Leach's word that this is their house and this is their stuff. And the entertainment factor was to watch as Leach showed off all these glamorous items that you could aspire to have yourself, knowing that you really were not ever going to be in a position to buy a million-dollar necklace or a five-hundred-dollar dish of caviar. People loved watching the show.

We live in a new Gilded Age, an age in which the prosperity theme comes back, and materialism becomes the warp and woof of the culture. But consumerism is as much a danger to our souls as anything we could possibly know. It is as much a threat to our families as anything we could possibly detect. Consumerism and materialism are as much a threat to our churches as any other heresy we might envision, any other sin we might understand. These sins come in to us with their false promises, and are so easily accepted by all of us.

Why are so many parents so distracted? Why are there so many latchkey children who come home to an empty house? All too often, it is because we live in a society that praises covetousness. Most of what we define as "necessary" has been defined by the warped expectations of the new Gilded Age—a completely artificial expectation.

Speaking statistically, the net reality is that families seem to be having fewer children. Why? Too often, the answer given is that the parents cannot afford more children, as if people in past times who had many children were wealthier than we are now. Do we even hear the illogic of what we are saying?

On another note, it is interesting to listen to the young person who walks up to an older believer and says, "You know, I am really turned off by the materialism of the established church. I am really turned off with its consumerist mentality, and that is why I'm out, over here doing ministry without the consumerism." Yet, he stands there with iPod wires around his neck and an iPhone in his hand. This is just a different expression of covetousness and consumerism. So, is it right to rail against consumerism and materialism? Of course. But it is really hard to do that with credibility unless we admit we are already in the web of materialism, already in the glue of the coveting culture.

Did you know that some parents now hire interior designers to create magnificent bedrooms for their adolescent children? Have you seen all the babies in designer clothes? The baby wears Prada. There is something really odd about putting this little creature in a horribly expensive outfit that will be so quickly outgrown. Maybe these parents can cut the little designer logo off and stitch it on the next thing.

You see, it is so easy to point at the covetousness of others, and to point at the consumerist failures of others. But this commandment is our story; we are deeply embedded in this. We are struck by this command. As the apostle Paul says in Romans 7:7–9, this command kills us because when we look here, we find ourselves so easily.

We should admit we are already in the web of materialism, already in the glue of the coveting culture.

Jesus said, "Do not lay up for yourselves treasures on earth." Rather we are to store up for ourselves "treasures in heaven, where neither moth nor rust destroys and where thieves do not break in and steal" (Matthew 6:19–20). Later, Jesus warned His disciples, saying, "Take care, and be on your guard against all coveteousness, for one's life does not consist in the abundance of his possessions" (Luke 12:15). Even in the midst of abundance, we think if we can just get to the next point, then we will be happy. A reporter asked the late John D. Rockefeller, one of America's richest men, how much money it takes to be satisfied. Rockefeller said, "One dollar more." And so it goes.

> *Riches* are deceitful because they steal the soul.

Jesus warns us about covetousness, saying that riches are deceitful because they steal the soul. And yet, there is a danger for us of misreading all this, thinking that the solution is to replace desire with *no* desire. That is Buddhism, not Christianity. Buddhism is about the renunciation of desire, and that is not the focus of the Tenth Commandment. Rather, the command focuses on replacing the *wrong* desire with the right desire. Violating the Tenth Commandment is actually a direct violation of the First Commandment. We are placing another god before us, the god of this object or the god of that consumer product or of this lifestyle or this or that aspiration. By God's grace, and by the same defying power of Word and spirit, we exchange a lesser desire for a greater desire, a temporal desire for an eternal desire, a corrupting desire for a sanctifying desire.

OUR HEART'S DESIRE

We are to desire Christ. We are to desire the glory of God. We are to desire fellowship with the one true and living God. We are to desire those things that are above. We are to desire heaven. And a part of what it means to desire heaven is to understand that there and there alone will our satisfaction be found. Here there can be no satisfaction, for our stuff can burn, get stolen, corrupt, dissipate, and be diminished. The very moment you drive your new car off the lot, it becomes a used car with a much lesser value than it had an hour earlier. Everything tends toward its own dissolution—moths eat it, rust destroys it, and thieves steal it.

We are not to renounce desire. Instead, we are to find the right desire and forfeit the wrong desire. We are to let go of the desire for material goods and earthly pleasures. These things can so easily eclipse our desire for the things of God. In Psalm 73:2–5, we find a wonderful testimony to this as the psalmist writes of how this became a snare for him. He says:

> But as for me, my feet had almost stumbled, my steps had nearly slipped. For I was envious of the arrogant when I saw the prosperity of the wicked. For they have no pangs until death; their bodies are fat and sleek. They are not in trouble as others are; they are not stricken like the rest of mankind.

It is so easy to do this, to envy the prosperity of others, even the wicked. People like to read about the rich and the famous, or to drive in rich neighborhoods and say, "These people must be happy. These people must be fulfilled. Their desires must be satisfied." But it just isn't so. There are actually problems the rich have that the poor can't even afford. There are pathologies of those who have too much that those who have too little will never understand.

Nevertheless, the Tenth Commandment levels humankind, because rich and poor alike covet.

In Psalm 73, we read an honest assessment made by the psalmist as he is confronted with his own covetousness. He finds that he has not renounced desire, yet he still desires God: "Whom have I in heaven but you? And there is nothing on earth that I desire besides you" (Psalm 73:25). This wise psalmist wants to forfeit one desire to embrace God as his true desire.

FEELING SAD

In Luke 18:18 a rich, young ruler approaches Jesus, asking him, "What must I do to inherit eternal life?" Jesus recites the commandments, and the man very easily says, "Well, I kept all those. Done. Went to Sabbath school. Raised by good Jewish parents" (paraphrase of verses 20–21). But then, Jesus shows him just how far short he falls of the commands. "One thing you still lack. Sell all that you [possess] and distribute to the poor, and you will have treasure in heaven; and come, follow me." Then Luke reports, "But when he heard these things, he became very sad, for he was extremely rich" (verses 22–23).

Indeed, the Tenth Commandment can bring sadness, because it nails us, forcing us to decide among the options. The rich young ruler went away sad, and this pictures for us the deceitfulness of riches. They can entrap the soul even unto death! When Jesus told him to sell all that he had and give it to the poor, Jesus was not giving him a new gospel of wealth redistribution. Instead, Jesus gave him a diagnostic test, like a CAT scan or an MRI of the soul, which revealed to this man that even as he claimed to be a lawkeeper, he was actually a lawbreaker. He was not willing to do what Christ commanded, and covetousness was at the heart of his refusal.

In Romans 7, Paul addresses himself to the law, making very clear that the law kills and cannot save. He then is very clear also to say that the law is nevertheless a gift. Paul says, "What then shall we say? That the law is sin? By no means! Yet if it had not been for the law, I would not have known sin. I would not have known what it is to covet if the law had not said, 'You shall not covet'" (Romans 7: 7).

Paul says that except for this command and for the specificity and moral force of it, we would not see coveting for what it is. We would explain it as something else, dressing it up as an appropriate desire. We would repackage it as a desire to do well, a way of career enhancement, a way of helping more people, of being a better steward with more rather than an inferior steward with less.

As Luther says, we can dress up our rascality. But the law gets to our heart, giving us this inner diagnosis and keeping us from delusion and spiritual blindness. Thus Paul insists that the law is actually grace to us. The law can't save, but it does diagnose the problem, getting to the heart of the issue and killing us. The law makes us realize what great sinners we are, so we can understand what a great Savior Christ is.

LIKE A VIRUS WITHIN

So, how bad is coveting, really? How insidious is it? I mean, what kind of deadly danger are we facing here? Calvin helps us here, saying, "For if by law, covetousness is not dragged from its lair, it destroys wretched men so secretly that they do not even feel its fatal stab."[3] It is that deadly. It is like a virus within us, and it is killing us when we don't even see it. It is there when we think it is dormant.

The great preacher John Chrysostom said, "Even more dangerous than sins of the flesh is the sin of covetousness." In effect, he is saying, "Look, even lust can be temporarily satisfied, but covetousness never is. It never sleeps. It never rests. Covetousness is the only sin that trumps lust." And we find this to be true in our own life.

In his *Confessions*, Augustine tells a story that gets right to the heart of this problem, and is probably the most famous account out of this great book, the first great Christian autobiography. Augustine gives this personal anecdote from his childhood:

> There was a pear tree near our vineyard laden with fruit. One stormy night, we rascally youth set out to rob it and carry our spoils away. We took off a huge load of pears, not to feast upon ourselves, but to throw them to the pigs, though we ate just enough to have pleasure of forbidden fruit. They were nice pears, but it was not the pears my wretched soul coveted, for I had plenty better at home. I picked them simply in order to become a thief. The only feast I got was a feast of iniquity. And that I enjoyed to the full. What was it that I loved in that theft? Was it the pleasure of acting against the law in order that I, a prisoner under rules, might have a maimed counterfeit of freedom by doing what was forbidden? The desire to steal was awakened simply by the prohibition of stealing. The pears were desirable simply because they were forbidden.[4]

How bad is coveting? So evil, so wretched, and so corrupting that it reaches the very center of the human heart—sin runs to the deepest level.

The same Hebrew word used in the Tenth Commandment in Exodus is also used in Genesis 3:6. Here in this passage about the fall, the primal sin is the same word—the wrong desire—"When the woman saw that the tree was good for food, and that it was a delight to the eyes, and that the tree was *to be desired* to make one wise, she took of its fruit and ate, and she also gave some to her husband who was with her, and he ate"(Genesis 3:6, italics added). Adam and Eve hankered after that which was forbidden, revealing to us just how basic and fundamental this sin is.

That is why we so desperately need this Tenth Commandment. It is a lifelong battle fought by the poor and the rich alike. And for the Christian minister, it is of even greater importance. John Newton said this: "Nothing is a greater bar to a minister's usefulness or renders his person and his labors more contemptible than a known attachment to money, a gripping fist and a hard heart." Speaking of the sin of covetousness, among ministers he said, "A day will come when mercenary preachers will wish they had begged their bread from door to door or had been chained to the oar of a galley for life rather than have presumed to intrude into the church such base and unworthy views."[5]

> *We* are so dependent upon the indwelling Spirit because the only means of rescue is from above.

This is an issue in the New Testament, where Paul speaks of Demas and says, "For Demas, in love with this present world, has deserted me and gone to Thessalonica" (2 Timothy 4:10). In Philemon 1:24, and in Colossians 4:14, Demas was with Paul. Along with Luke and Paul, Demas greeted the saints where the letters were written there to Colossae and to Philemon. Paul recognizes Demas's companionship during an awful period of persecution, even in Roman imprisonment. And yet, even as Paul's life is nearing its end, Demas deserted him because of the love of the things of the world.

Once again, we are not talking about a renunciation of desire. We are talking about the exchange of desire—lesser for greater, lower for higher, temporal for an eternal. We are to love the Lord our God with all of our heart and soul and mind, and we are to love our neighbor as ourself—and all this is possible only if we renounce our own desires in order to follow the lordship of Christ.

There is grace that we would know this. There is grace that even as the law kills, it tells us of our need as Christians. We are not called to less than Israel was commanded in the Ten Commandments, we are called to more. If the tenth commandment goes to the interior, then we understand that for those who follow Christ, His lordship gets even closer to the interior. And this is why we so desperately need the Word. This is why we are so dependent upon the indwelling Spirit, because the only means of rescue is from above.

We cannot free ourselves from the society in which we live. We cannot blind ourselves to the advertisements, to the commercials, and to the billboards. We cannot ignore our neighbors. We understand these things are going on and the bent of our hearts is toward covetousness. The lie that deludes and deceives so many will deceive us as well, but for the Spirit of God within us and the ministry of the Word of God to us. So it will be till we reach the end.

BY HIS MERCY, BY HIS GRACE

We reach the conclusion of the Ten Commandments with the knowledge that it is only by God's mercy that we would ever know such truths. It is only by divine grace that we can hear such wisdom from our Creator. In His mercy, God does not leave us to our own sinful devices, but instead He lovingly commands us.

As Christians, we read these commandments with the knowledge that, more than anything else, these commandments point to Jesus Christ as the fulfillment of the law and the prophets. Understood rightly, these commandments lead, not to our despair that we fall short of them, but to our thankfulness for the gospel of Jesus Christ.

Christ comes to save lawbreakers like ourselves. Thus, we see the commandments themselves as grace to us. But our confidence is not in our ability to keep these commandments, for we will surely fail. Our confidence is in Christ, whose perfect obedience fulfills the law.

The Ten Commandments, first heard by Israel as the covenant people of God, are now heard by the church of the Lord Jesus Christ. We are instructed by the law as we cling to the gospel of Christ.

𝒩otes

INTRODUCTION: HAS ANY PEOPLE HEARD THE VOICE OF GOD SPEAKING . . . AND SURVIVED?

1. Eugene Merrill, *Deuteronomy*, New American Commentary (Nashville: Broadman & Holman, 1994), 130–31.

2. Christopher J. H. Wright, *Deuteronomy*, New International Biblical Commentary (Peabody, Mass.: Hendrickson, 1996), 55.

3. Francis A. Schaeffer, *The Francis A. Schaeffer Trilogy* (Wheaton, Ill.: Good News Publishers, 1990), 158–60.

4. Carl F. H. Henry, *God Who Speaks and Shows*, vol. 3 of *God, Revelation and Authority* (Wheaton, Ill.: Crossway, 1999), 405.

5. Ibid.

6. Jonathan Edwards, "A History of the Work of Redemption," vol. 5 of *The Works of President Edwards* (London: Hughes and Baynes, 1817), 54–55.

7. John H. Sammis and Daniel B. Towner, "Trust and Obey," *The Baptist Hymnal* (Nashville: Convention Press, 1991). In public domain.

CHAPTER 1: NO OTHER GOD, NO OTHER VOICE

1. Jonathan Edwards, "Inquiry Concerning Qualification for Communion," in *The Works of President Edwards*, vol. 1 (New York: Leavitt & Allen, 1858), 160.

2. Piotr Bienkowski and Alan Millard, eds., *Dictionary of the Ancient Near East* (Philadelphia: Univ. of Pennsylvania, 2000), 90.

3. "Now, A Few Words from the Wise," Time, 22 June 1987.

4. "Break Glass in Case of Emergency," in *Beyond the Boom: New Voices on American Life, Culture, and Politics*, ed. Terry Teachout (New York: Poseidon, 1990), 49–62.

5. Herbert Schlossberg, *Idols for Destruction* (Wheaton, Ill.: Crossway, 1993), 6.

6. A. W. Tozer, *The Knowledge of the Holy* (New York: HarperOne, 1978), 1–2.

7. James Orr, *The Christian View of God and the World as Centering in the Incarnation* (Edinburgh: Morrison and Gibb, 1893), 422–24.

8. Philip Graham Ryken, *Written in Stone* (Wheaton, Ill.: Crossway, 2003), 58.

9. Gore Vidal, *The Decline and Fall of the American Empire* (Berkeley, Calif.: Odonian, 1992), 77.

CHAPTER 2: THE GOD WHO IS HEARD AND NOT SEEN

1. Roger Scruton, *The Aesthetics of Music* (New York: Oxford Univ. Press, 1999), 460.

2. Walter Chalmers Smith, "Immortal, Invisible, God Only Wise" in *The Baptist Hymnal* (Nashville: Convention Press, 1998), 11. In public domain.

3. Mitchell Stephens, *The Rise of the Image, the Fall of the Word* (New York: Oxford Univ. Press, 1998), 11.

4. Neil Postman, *Amusing Ourselves to Death* (New York: Penguin, 1985), 9.

5. Raymond C. Ortlund Jr., *Whoredom: God's Unfaithful Wife in Biblical Theology* (Grand Rapids: Eerdmans, 1996).

CHAPTER 3: HONORING THE GOD WE KNOW BY NAME

1. "Be Careful Little Eyes." In public domain; http://www.whereincity.com/india-kids/rhymes/84.

2. Augustine's "Two Loves" are described in Allan Fitzgerald and John C. Cavadini, *Augustine Through the Ages: An Encyclopedia* (Grand Rapids: Eerdmans, 1999), 28–29.

3. Friedrich Wilhelm Nietzsche, *The Antichrist* (Whitefish, Mont.: Kessinger 2004), 12.

4. David Van Biema and Jeff Chu, "Does God Want You to Be Rich?" *Time*, 10 September 2006.

5. A. W. Tozer, *Worship: The Missing Jewel* (repr.; Camp Hill, Pa.: Christian Publications, 1992).

6. A. W. Tozer, sermon, "Complete Surrender"; see "Tozer on entertainment 04," at http://www.propheticcollege.wordpress.com/category/tozer-onentertainment/.

7. Stephen L. Carter, *God's Name in Vain: The Wrongs and Rights of Religion in Politics* (New York: Basic, 2001), 12–13.

8. John Calvin, *Institutes of the Christian Religion*, 2.8.22, ed. John T. McNeil, trans. Ford Lewis Battles, Library of Christian Classics (Philadelphia: Westminster, 2001), 388.

CHAPTER 4: RESTING SECURE IN THE GOD WHO SAVES US

1. Geerhardus Vos, *Biblical Theology* (Grand Rapids: Eerdmans, 1948; repr., Carlisle, Pa.: The Banner of Truth Trust, 2004), 138–43.

2. *The Westminster Confession of Faith*, XXI, section 8.

CHAPTER 5: HONORING OUR PARENTS, CHERISHING A PATRIMONY

1. Christopher J. H. Wright, *Deuteronomy*, New International Biblical Commentary (Peabody, Mass.: Hendrickson Publishers, 1996), 77.

2. John Calvin, *Institutes of the Christian Religion*, 2.8.35–38, ed. John T. McNeil,

trans. Ford Lewis Battles, vol. 2 (Philadelphia: Westminster Press, 2001), 401–404.

3. Charles Hodge, *Systematic Theology*, vol. 3 (New York: Scribner's, 1872–73; repr., Grand Rapids: Eerdmans, 1940), 349.

4. Saint Augustine of Hippo, *Essential Sermons: The Works of Saint Augustine*, ed. Daniel Doyle, trans. Edmund Hill (Hyde Park, N.Y.: New City Press, 2007), 31.

5. Jane English, "What Do Grown Children Owe Their Parents?" in *Aging and Ethics*, ed. Nancy S. Jecker (Nashville: The Humana Press, 1991), 147.

CHAPTER 6: THE SANCTITY OF LIFE AND THE VIOLENCE OF SIN

1. Eric Hobsbawm, *The Age of Extremes* (New York: Random House, 1994).

2. Winston Churchill, *The World Crisis, 1911–1918* (New York: Free Press, 2005), 4.

3. Wilma Ann Bailey, *"You Shall Not Kill" or "You Shall Not Murder"?: The Assault on a Biblical Text* (Collegeville, Minn: Liturgical Press, 2005), 22–23.

4. *I am the Lord Your God*, ed. Carl E. Braaten and Christopher R. Seitz (Grand Rapids: Eerdmans, 2005), 127–47.

CHAPTER 7: WHY ADULTERY IS ABOUT MUCH MORE THAN SEX

1. Stephen Kiehl, "Adulterers Need Cards Too," *Los Angeles Times*, 12 July 2005; on the Internet at http.//www.articles.latimes.com/2005/jul/12/entertainment/et-cards12

2. Raymond C. Ortlund, Jr. *Whoredom: God's Unfaithful Wife in Biblical Theology* (Grand Rapids: Eerdmans, 1996), 25.

CHAPTER 8: DEALING WITH THE INNER EMBEZZLER

1. Martin Luther, *The Large Catechism of Martin Luther*, trans. Robert H. Fischer (Minneapolis: Augsburg Fortress, 1963), 40.

2. Winston Churchill, *Winston S. Churchill: His Complete Speeches, 1897–1963*, vol. 7, ed. Robert Rhodes James (New York: Chelsea House Publishers, 1974), 566.

3. Charles Hodge, *Systematic Theology*, vol. 3, (Peabody, Mass: Hendrickson, 1999), 421.

CHAPTER 9: THE TRUTH, THE WHOLE TRUTH, AND NOTHING BUT THE TRUTH

1. Friedrich Nietzsche, "On Truth and Lies in a Nonmoral Sense," *Philosophy and Truth: Selections from Nietzsche's Notebooks of the Early 1870s.* trans. and ed. Daniel Breazeale (Atlantic Highlands, N.J.: Humanities Press, 1979), 86.

2. Bob Minzesheimer, "James Frey Takes a Novel Approach with 'Bright Shiny Morning,'" *USA Today*, 12 May 2008; as accessed at www.usatoday.com/life/books/news/2008-05-12-james-frey-N.htm.

3. Marcelle Clements, "Truth About Lying," *Child*, April 2005.

4. James Petigru Boyce, "Three Changes in Theological Institutions," accessed 4 March 2009, http://www.founders.org/library/three.html.

5. Saint Augustine, "On Lying" and "Against Lying" in *Treatises on Various Subjects*, ed. Roy J. Deferrari (New York, 1952).

6. David Jablonsky, *Churchill, the Great Game and Total War* (New York: Routledge, 1991), 172.

CHAPTER 10: WHY COVETEOUSNESS KILLS CONTENTMENT

1. Martin Luther, *The Large Catechism of Martin Luther*, trans. Robert H. Fischer (Minneapolis: Augsburg Fortress, 1963), 49.

2. Andrew Fuller, *The Works of the Rev. Andrew Fuller*, vol. 4 (New Haven, Conn.: Converse, 1824), 362.

3. John Calvin, *Institutes of the Christian Religion* (1559; repr. Louisville, Kent.: Westminister John Knox, 1960), 355.

4. Augustine, *Confessions*, II.IV.

5. Rev. Richard Cecil, *The Works of the Reverend John Newton* (London: Hamilton, Adams, and Co, 1824), 236.

HE IS NOT SILENT

ISBN-13: 978-0-8024-5489-8

FOREWORD BY JOHN MACARTHUR

HE IS NOT SILENT

(((⊥)))

PREACHING IN A
POSTMODERN WORLD

R. ALBERT MOHLER, JR.

"Contemporary preaching suffers from a loss of confidence in the power of the Word . . . from an infatuation with technology . . . from an embarrassment before the biblical text . . . from an evacuation of biblical content . . . from a focus on felt needs . . . from an absence of gospel . . ."

In this powerful book, *He is not Silent: Preaching in a Postmodern World*, Mohler shows us how. In a style both commanding and encouraging, Mohler lays the groundwork for preaching, fans the flame on the glory of preaching, and calls out with an urgent need for preaching. This message is desperately needed yet not often heard. Whether you're concerned or enthused by the state of the church today, join Mohler as he examines preaching and why the church can't survive without it.

1-800-678-8812 • MOODYPUBLISHERS.COM